BY THE WAY 2

By the way 2
A selection of public art in Ireland

Ann Lane

Wordwell

First published in 2019 by

Wordwell Ltd
Unit 9
78 Furze Road
Sandyford Industrial Estate
Dublin 18
Eircode: D18 C6V6
www.wordwellbooks.com

While every effort has been made by the author and publisher to identify the artists and the title of their works, it has not in all cases been possible to do so with absolute certainty. Any errors that may have occurred will be corrected in later editions of this book.

ISBN 978-1-9164922-8-8

Book design: Nick Maxwell and Niamh Power

Copy-editing: Emer Condit

Cover design: Ger Garland

Cover: *The Irish Elk*, Clare Bigger and Paul Regan.
Bó Bainne, Lynn Kirkham and Cathal O'Meara Landscape Architects

Printed by: Gráficas Castuera, Pamplona

CONTENTS

DEDICATION

To the sculptors and the artist blacksmiths whose dedication to their art enhances the landscape for the rest of us. I hope that I have done justice to their talents.

Also dedicated to the memory of my friend, Noel Whelan, who was so supportive of all my projects.

ACKNOWLEDGEMENTS

Nothing is ever achieved in isolation; to some degree everything is a team effort, and I have very many people to thank for their part in this project.

First of all there are the people and organisations who provided financial assistance—Teagasc, McKeon Stone, the late Feargal Quinn, Norma Smurfit and Lochlann Quinn. I am indebted to them for their support of the arts by action as well as words. Special thanks to Professor Gerry Boyle, Frank Buckley, Susan McElroy, Anne Lyons and Bairbre Murray.

I am grateful to the following for permission to extract information from their public art brochures: Músaem Chorca Dhuibhne for the excellent Dingle and West Sculpture Trail brochure, and in particular Isabel Bennett, who gave me so much of her time; Sneem Tidy Towns; Elaine Murphy of the Roe Valley Arts and Cultural Centre for the Limavady Sculpture Trail brochure; Martin Carey, Chief Executive, Mourne Heritage Trust, for the Mourne and Ring of Gullion Public Art Trail brochure; and Dundalk Tidy Towns Committee for the Arts Walk Trail brochure.

For their hospitality in their homes my thanks to Michael and Gerry Harty, Madge Duffy, Jim and Noreen Hamilton, Aidan Gray and his parents, Michael and Rosaleen Keohane, Brooke Bremner and David Glueck. For helping me to find sculptures in their areas I want to thank Rita Curran, Michael Lee, Mary O'Riordan, Margaret Sweetnam, Anne Cowman, Mary Reardon and Irene Berry.

For their help in a variety of ways I am grateful to Ursula Quill and Charlie Larkin, Trish Brennan, Vera Ryan, Redmond O'Riain, David Lane, Rina Whyte, Noel McDonald, Norman Dungan, Irene Martin, Barbara Hussey for her invaluable assistance, Catherine Walsh in Cork and her daughter Nuala, her Dublin rep! My thanks also to Denise Maguire for being my guide around Omagh and Strabane, and to herself, Conor and Sarah for the fun in their home; to Paul Clements of the *Irish Times* for his precise directions to Manannán Mac Lir at the spectacular Gortmore viewing point, which I would have missed out on if left to my own devices; and to Eddie Doherty, in his beautiful Donegal tweed shop, for his help in Ardara. The shop is well worth a visit to see Eddie working on a traditional loom.

I very much appreciate the helpfulness of library staff all over the country. My thanks to County Council Arts Officers and Arts Office staff who responded to my queries: Jenny Sherwin, Mary Mullins, Mary Brady, Clare Dunne, Denis Darcy, Ciara King and Therese McKenna.

In Northern Ireland I was greatly assisted by Rosalind Lowry and Jayne Clarke, Mid and East Antrim Borough Council; Bernard Clarkson, Samantha Curry and Karen Smyth, Antrim and Newtownabbey Borough Council; Elaine Gaston, Causeway Coast and Glens Borough Council; Bernie Kirrane and Diane Henshaw, Fermanagh and Omagh District Council; Leah Duncan, Armagh City, Banbridge and Craigavon Borough Council; Seamus Crossey, Newry, Mourne and Down District Council; and Mandy McAvoy and Camilla Fitzpatrick, Mourne Heritage Trust.

I am really delighted that John Sheahan of The Dubliners allowed me to include his poem 'Digital Snapshot', and my thanks to Harriet for facilitating it. My own personal proofreader and sounding-board has, as always, been a constant support. And, of course, my enduring thanks to Nick Maxwell and his wife Una MacConville, as well as Helen Dunne and Nick's entire team at Wordwell Books, for the care and attention they have lavished on this project—and, indeed, on all my previous efforts. This is the last one, I promise!

If I have omitted to mention anybody I am truly sorry, but be assured that your help was valued and much appreciated.

Ann Lane
January 2019

FOREWORD

The great tradition of public art on our island is no recent phenomenon but reaches back thousands of years to a time when the earliest inhabitants first raised the megaliths and ancient monuments which can still be found across our country. In medieval Ireland the people erected high crosses and standing stones, physical manifestations of their new faith. Over the past two centuries the neo-classical representations of British monarchs gradually gave way to statutes venerating the men and women of our revolutionary generation and celebrations of our long and difficult struggle for independence.

Over the past 30 years a new wave of public art has been made possible by the commitment of citizens in towns and villages across Ireland, and most importantly by national policy through the Per Cent for Art Scheme. The diverse sculptures which now grace our countryside are a testament not only to the creativity and innovation of the individual artist but also to the power of collective action to adequately fund and sustain public art. As this wonderful collection demonstrates, the new public art, though informed and sustained by ancient tradition, has not bound itself to old conventions.

Great art should be not only rewarded but also recorded, so we must all be very grateful to Ann Lane for assembling this marvellous index of sculptures. For those fortunate enough to live and travel in Ireland it can provide a new perspective on our native landscape and our journeys through it. For those who have never come to our country I trust that it will arouse curiosity and interest. I hope that all those who open this book will find it as inspiring as I have.

Michael D. Higgins
President of Ireland

DIGITAL SNAPSHOT

Through the camera's watchful eye
A fleeting moment is halted,
Fragmented, and coded for retrieval
In a gallery where pictures
Hang weightless on memory hooks.

In this bank of time
When the past is primed for recall,
Captive moments, reprieved and refreshed,
Come flashing back
In a digital dance of pixels.

INTRODUCTION

In 2010 Wordwell Books published *By the way*, my photographic record of many of the public sculptures that adorn our countryside. As time passed, I realised that there were installations that I was not aware of when I was researching that book, as well as much new work. So in 2017 I set out to record these pieces, and this collection of more than 1,000 images is the result of my efforts.

As before, the purpose of this book is to showcase the range of works displayed on roadsides, roundabouts, motorways, towns and villages the length and breadth of the country. As the project evolved, I realised that, because of the quantity, I had to set some limits on what I would include, so apart from a few token pieces I have excluded cities. With regard to Dublin, there are already two very helpful publications: Neal Doherty's *The complete guide to the statues and sculptures of Dublin City* (Orpen Press, 2015) and Muriel Bolger's *Statues and stories: Dublin's monuments unveiled* (Ashfield Press, 2006).

Because I have concentrated on contemporary installations, much of the art included in both of my books exists because of the Per Cent for Art Scheme, whereby a government decision in 1997 approved the inclusion in the budgets for public bodies delivering capital programmes of up to 1% as funding for public art, subject to certain limits. I didn't restrict myself in any way, however; as far as I was concerned, a permanent outdoor piece in a public place qualified for inclusion, irrespective of who commissioned it. When you see the images in this book, I think you will agree that the quality—never mind the quantity—of public art in this country is exceptional, and we are fortunate indeed to have such talented artists living and working here.

I found it disappointing that there are so many sculptures all over the place that don't have information plaques—the title and the artist's name would do. This basic information would be of special interest to visitors from abroad, who might not know the significance of a specific piece in relation to the history or legend of where it is sited. In my view it's like buying a book without knowing the title or the author's name.

Travelling the length and breadth of Ireland in pursuit of this project was a unique, educational and sometimes entertaining experience. There was always the unexpected: the casual mention in a local shop of the Evie Hone window in a small country church; the Crete Boom concrete ship near Ballina; the spot near Tralee where Scotia, the daughter of an Egyptian pharaoh, is reputed to be buried; the photogenic *Bád Eddie* wreck on Magheraclogher beach near Gweedore; taking a break in the South Pole Inn in Annascaul, the pub once owned by my great hero, Antarctic explorer Tom Crean; almost walking over the cliff edge when I was looking for the Baltimore beacon in heavy fog; strolling through the Dark Hedges and visiting the castle in Antrim where parts of the popular series *Game of Thrones* was filmed, while never actually having seen an episode myself!

I drove 34,500km, and the more I saw the more I was reminded yet again of what a sensational country this is. We have an extraordinary diversity of landscape, some of it quite breathtaking. There are drives like Glencolmcille/Ardara, Belmullet/Blacksod Pier, Slea Head/Brandon Point, Pilltown/Mullinavat, the Windyhill Road, Coleraine/Limavady and the Warrenpoint/Newcastle coast road. I am now looking forward to travelling the country again at a more leisurely pace to take in the very many special sights that I had to whizz past in pursuit of the project.

I hope you will find this collection of the public sculptures of the country as interesting as recording them was for me, and that it will encourage you to undertake your own journeys to enjoy them as much as I did.

Ann Lane
January 2019

PROFILE

Photo: Tony Maxwell

Ann Lane was born and educated in Millstreet, Co. Cork, and has lived in Dublin for most of her life.

She worked as personal assistant to Mary Robinson for 28 years during her time as lawyer, European Law lecturer in Trinity College Dublin, senator and then president of Ireland. Subsequently she spent ten years as personal assistant to three attorneys general: David Byrne, Michael McDowell and the late Rory Brady. Prior to retirement she worked for ten years with Senator Ivana Bacik in Leinster House.

Travel has been an abiding interest—from both the North and South Polar regions to very many captivating places in between!

PREVIOUS PUBLICATIONS

By the way: a selection of public art in Ireland (Wordwell Books, 2010).

The moment and the day: archives and anecdotes (Wordwell Books, 2014).

Photographic work included in *Art and architecture of Ireland* (Yale University Press/Royal Irish Academy/Paul Mellon Centre, 2014).

Connacht

MACHNAMH
1916 Memorial Park, Athenry
Sculpture of the Irish mythological hero Cúchulainn, unveiled on Easter Monday 2016 and commemorating the 1916 Easter Rising.
Jethro Sheen

FIELDS OF ATHENRY
Town Park, Athenry
Donnacha Cahill

COMMEMORATIVE GARDEN
Swan Gate, Athenry
Stone carving depicting an eviction in the late nineteenth century.
Cormac O'Reilly

SEATS
Town Park and Cross Street, Athenry
Two of several seats spread about the town.
Donnacha Cahill

SCÁILEANNA NA MBÁD / THE SHADOWS OF THE BOATS
Trá an Dóilín, Coral Strand, An Cheathrú, Carraroe
Stainless steel and black resin group sculpture inspired by the currachs, black-sailed hookers and other vessels of Connemara.
Edward Delaney

ALCOCK AND BROWN MONUMENT
Derrygimlagh Bog, Clifden
The installation, in the shape of a tail fin, commemorates British aviators John Alcock and Arthur Brown, who made the first non-stop transatlantic flight in 1919. They flew their modified WWI Vickers Vimy bomber from St John's in Newfoundland, making landfall on the bog near the Marconi Wireless Station on 15 June after less than sixteen hours' flying time.
Artist's name unknown to the author

THE RIFLE

Main Square, Clifden

Bronze piece commemorating the St Patrick's Battalion, the *San Patricios*, formed and led by John Riley, who fought against the United States in the Mexican–American War of 1846–8.

Sebastian

In the background is An Rabhcán / The Beacon, by Declan Breen.

ABOUT FISHERS OF MEN

Woods Walk, Cong

Across the bridge from the County Mayo village (the river divides the counties), the installation incorporates the Gospel of Matthew with the sea-god of Celtic mythology, Manannán Mac Lir, who commands the boat passages between the sun and the voyages into the underworld.

Travis Price

1940s CRAUGHWELL
Main Street, Craughwell
Orlagh Fahy

FURBO VILLAGE

Mick Wilkins

LILY
Limestone, marble, bronze and gold leaf, commemorating the 1916 Rising.

ANGEL
Life-size figure in a memorial garden.

DOVE
Bronze.

1916 COMMEMORATIVE HARP
County Hall, Prospect Hill, Galway
Part of the 1916 Centenary programme.
Jethro Sheen

OSCAR WILDE
William Street, Galway
Bronze of Oscar and Estonian writer Eduard Wilde on a granite bench. This is a replica of a statue in Tartu, Estonia. It was gifted to Galway city by the Estonian people in 2004, marking Estonia's membership of the European Union that year. Cast from the original sculpture by Tiiu Kirsipuu at the Wilde Irish Pub in Tartu.

CLADDAGH ICON
Fr Griffin Road, Galway
John Coll

PLAQUE
Wolfe Tone Bridge, Galway
Poem by Moya Cannon entitled "Bright City".
Pádraic Reaney

COLUMBUS MONUMENT
The Claddagh, Galway
Commemorating Christopher Columbus's visit to Galway around 1477—he mentions the city in his writings.
Mick Wilkins

MEMORIAL TO SEAMEN
Claddagh Basin, Galway
Stone monument with stylised bird, a tribute to eight Claddagh fishermen who lost their lives in May 1902 when a squall capsized their boat on the way home from a wedding.
Mick Wilkins

BULRUSHES
Community School, Glenamaddy
Stainless steel, LED lighting and landscaping.
Alex Pentek

HARE

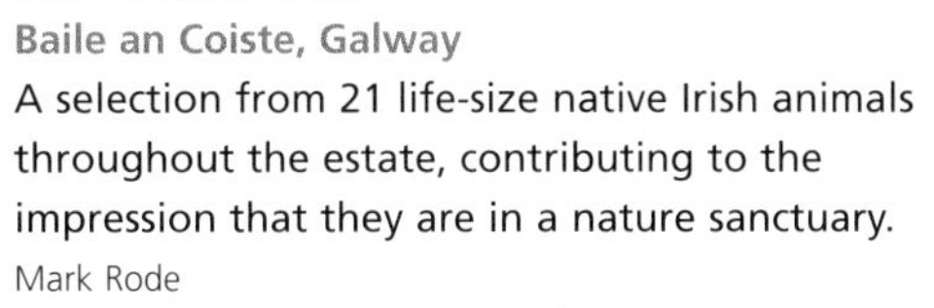

THE SANCTUARY

Baile an Coiste, Galway

A selection from 21 life-size native Irish animals throughout the estate, contributing to the impression that they are in a nature sanctuary.

Mark Rode

OTTER

BRENT GEESE

RED DEER FAWN

RED SQUIRRELS

THE INQUISITIVE HARE
Scoil Náisiúnta Iomair, Killimor
The hare stands on a stack of books that have designs on the spines. These are based on the events, the stories and experiences of the pupils and teachers who suggested them, relating to the school.
Donnacha Cahill

FISHERMAN IN BOAT, FISH AND HERON
Monearmore Roundabout, Loughrea
Donnacha Cahill

CHROMATIC SOUNDS
St Raphael's College, Cross Street, Loughrea
A two-day workshop with students led to the design of the artwork, and their drawings expressed their ability to hear colour and see music, to connect geometric shapes and colours to the rhythms of instrumental pieces by Ravel and Mozart. These outcomes were then taken by the artist to finalise the artwork that covers the school walls.
Marisa Ferreira

TAIRSEACH AN EOLAIS / THRESHOLD OF KNOWLEDGE
Gaelscoil Riabhach, Cois Móna, Loughrea
The open doors portray the energy of people coming and going through the school. A pathway of bronze stars leads through the piece to the school's main door. The stars symbolise the children's journey through school, inspired by Brendan the Navigator, who is the patron saint of Loughrea cathedral.
Fiona Coffey

BOBBYJO
Mountbellew
Bobbyjo, an Irish-bred racehorse, won the Irish Grand National in 1998 and the Aintree Grand National in 1999. On both occasions he was ridden by Paul Carberry, son of the horse's trainer, Tommy Carberry.
John Coll

ENDA COLLERAN
Moylough
A member of the Galway senior inter-county team from 1961 until 1971, Enda Colleran captained Galway to back-to-back All-Ireland titles in 1965 and 1966, and was later manager of the team.
John Coll

CEILLIÚRAGH / CELEBRATION
NUI Galway, near Bailey Allen Theatre
Monument to the Graduates' Association.
John Coll

GALWAY YELLOW
NUI Galway Library plaza
Painted steel piece, described by the artist as a derivation of the Celtic knot and unsurprisingly sometimes known by students as 'the big yellow thing'.
Brian King

CONNEMARA

Recess

No one can say that they do not have a sense of humour in Recess. The plaque reads: 'Conn the son of the sea. Built in 1999 by Joyce Craft Shop for no apparent reason'. The stone pyramid at the rear bears the legend: 'On this site in 1897 nothing happened'. Who cares if nothing happened here—it's a very beautiful spot and the locals have the best attitude!

Joyce's Craft Shop

VOYAGE OF DISCOVERY

Gaelscoil Dara, Br Bhaile an Lochain, Renmore

This piece references reading, sport, drama and the history of the school. Two boys and two girls set out on their own voyage.

Michael Disley

DONKEY AND CART
Bishop Street bridge, Tuam
Donnacha Cahill

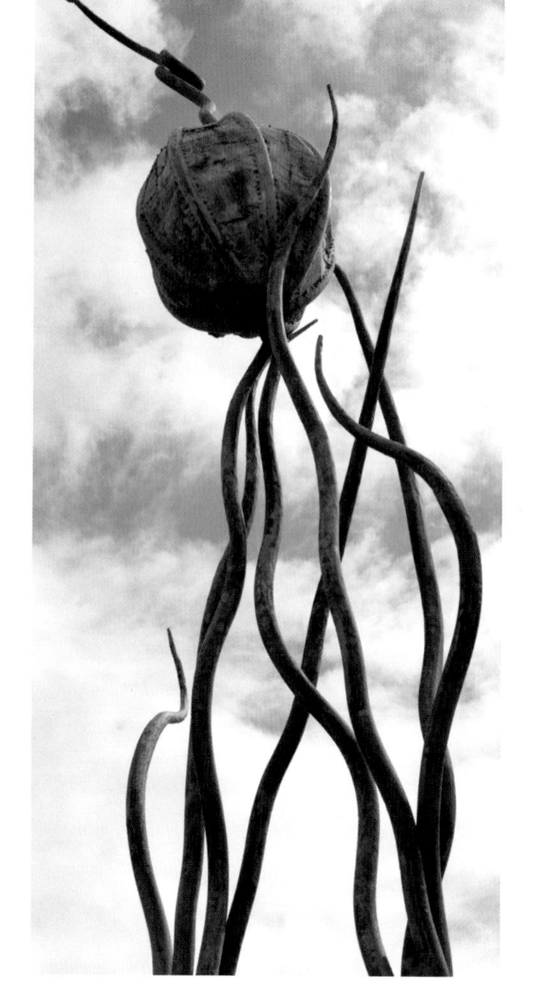

GERMINATING SEED
Beside the church, Tuam
Donnacha Cahill

GALWAY HOOKER
Eyre Square, Galway
Corten steel and limestone, celebrating a boat that was designed for fishing and was unique to the Galway Bay area.
Éamonn O'Doherty

MUTTON LIGHT FAMINE SHIP MEMORIAL
Grattan Beach, Salthill
The lighthouse in the distance is Mutton Light, the last point in the country seen by the many thousands of refugees who fled the Great Famine from the port of Galway in 1847–50. The memorial is dedicated to the captains and crews who carried them, and bears the names of 100 of their ships.
Artist's name unknown to the author

Leitrim

WIND HARPS

Beside the river, Carrick-on-Shannon

Four wind harps in stainless steel and titanium. The sounds are activated by the winds on the river.

Mark Garry

MOSAICS
Opposite County Council offices, Carrick-on-Shannon
Artist's name unknown to the author

MARGARET OF NEW ORLEANS
Health Centre, Carrigallen
The plaque on the Health Centre wall commemorates Margaret Gaffney, who was born in Tully in 1813. Her family emigrated to the US and she became famous in New Orleans for her dedication to housing children orphaned by yellow fever. She received a state funeral in 1882 and became the first woman in the US to have a statue erected in her honour, on a street now named Margaret's Place in New Orleans.
Fred Conlon

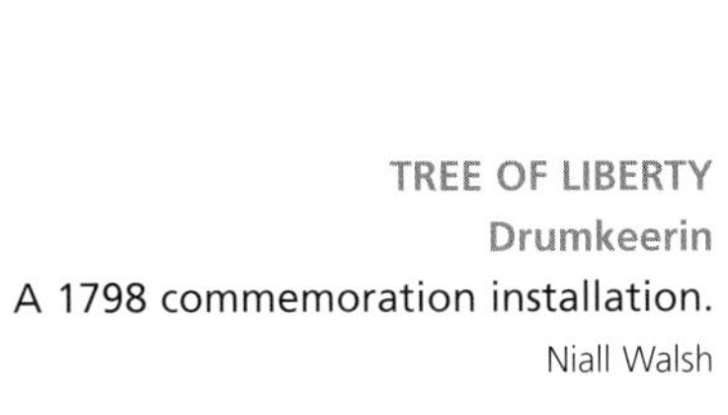

TREE OF LIBERTY
Drumkeerin
A 1798 commemoration installation.
Niall Walsh

TOM DUNPHY

Annaduff

Memorial to the Royal Showband's popular singer and musician, who was killed in a traffic accident here in 1975. Cyril and Adrian Smith and Des Shanley were involved in the excellent restoration of the piece for the 40th anniversary of Tom's death.

Jimmy Joe McKiernan

TURLOUGH O'CAROLAN

Market Square, Mohill

Commemorating the famous piper and composer, who was born in 1670 in Meath but spent some time living in Mohill.

Oisín Kelly

FOUR MASTERS MONUMENT
River Drowes bridge, Mullinaleck, Kinlough
In the Franciscan House at Drowes in 1632–6 these four men compiled the Annals of the Four Masters, recording the history of Ireland up to 1616.
James McKenna

Mayo

ACHILLHENGE
Keel, Achill Island
Modern concrete Stonehenge-type structure. I went to this installation determined to be outraged, but to my astonishment I found it strangely compelling. You can decide for yourself.
Joe McNamara

FLOW
Pearse Street, Ballina
Stainless steel, copper, bronze and polyurethane resin.
Joe Neeson

INSTINCT
Riverside walkway, Ballina
Cast-bronze, cast-glass, stainless steel piece, with an off-white patination. Resembles a fishing float and references the town's association with the salmon.
Rachel Joynt

BRADÁNACH / SALMON
Gurteens Roundabout, Ballina
Stainless steel leaping fish, inset with 50 small salmon shapes that give the piece the scaly effect of a fish.
John Hogan

THE ROLLING CAST
Foxford Road, Ballina
A mild steel abstract depiction of a person fishing to celebrate the graceful art of fly fishing.
John Hogan

HORSE BENCH
An Cladrach, Ballinrobe
Oak bench with carved backrest in the green area at the housing estate.
Walter Michael

SALMON
An Cladrach, Ballinrobe
Oak, slate and earthwork: carved fish at the estate's entrance.
Walter Michael

FOCAL EIGSE
Library, Main Street, Ballinrobe
Concrete blocks with ceramic finish; two overlaid large-scale book forms.
Marion O'Donnell

MOTHER AND CHILD
Ballintubber Abbey
Modelled on the statue of 'Our Lady of Ballintubber' made in 1973 by Professor Haerken of the National College of Art in Dublin.
Brother Joseph McNally, Singapore

UNTITLED

Aisling Drive, Ballyhaunis

Steel and bronze pillar.

Michael Burke

POINTS OF VIEW

St Gerald's Court, Ballyhaunis

Large stones decorated with abstract patterns. The largest one has a reflective surface on which the church across the road is visible in distorted form in reverse.

Remco de Fouw

EXILES MEMORIAL
Ballyvary
Bronze column with birds.
Colm Brennan

TRANSITION
Belmullet
Bronze piece showing the swans in the myth of the Children of Lir.
Paul Devlin

SLEÁN
Bárr na Trá
The implement used in the past to cut turf in the bogs.
Micky Monaghan

OPEN BOOK
Town centre, Belmullet
The bronze book is one of several pieces forming a sort of storyboard in a heritage trail around the town. This page is headed 'Planned Town—streetscape'. Texts provided by Belmullet Tidy Towns, fabricated by Callow bronze foundry.

INISHKEA CURRACH
Blacksod Peninsula
Paul Devlin and John Monaghan

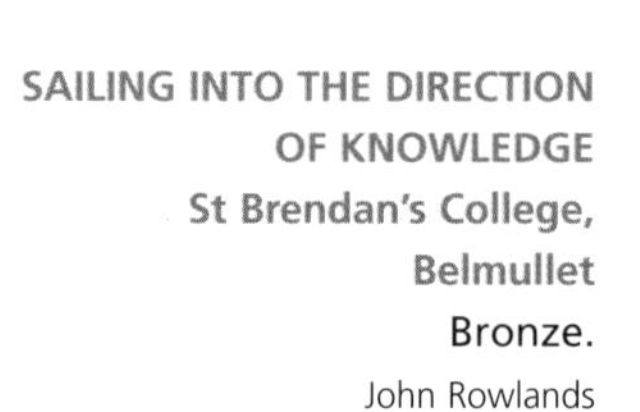

SAILING INTO THE DIRECTION OF KNOWLEDGE
St Brendan's College, Belmullet
Bronze.
John Rowlands

BATTLING FORCES
Downpatrick Headland
Lacken sandstone and uncut limestone, symbol of the forces of nature versus man-made elements.
Fritze Rind

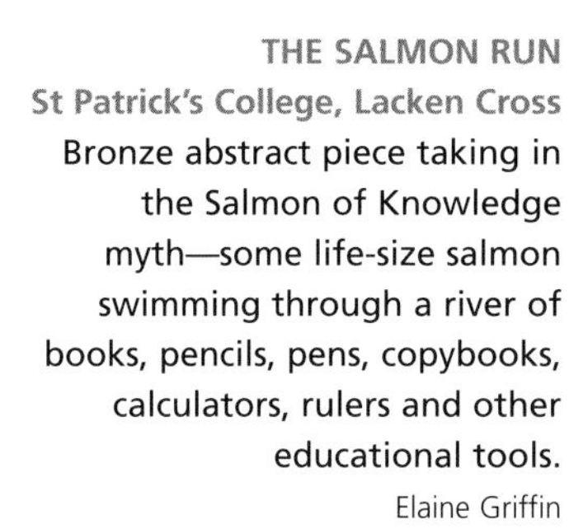

THE SALMON RUN
St Patrick's College, Lacken Cross
Bronze abstract piece taking in the Salmon of Knowledge myth—some life-size salmon swimming through a river of books, pencils, pens, copybooks, calculators, rulers and other educational tools.
Elaine Griffin

THIN PLACES
Dún na mBó / Doonamoe, Belmullet
The installation surrounds a blow-hole in a thrilling environment.
Travis Price

THE LAND EATING THE SEA
Ceann an Éanaigh / Annagh Head, Belmullet
Inspired by the early monastic beehives, the project is 'a refuge on the one hand, but also a vista celebrating the peninsula's eating of the sea'. I did not feel that this installation enhanced its spectacular surroundings.
Travis Price

TEMPLE OF THE TIDES
Belmullet Harbour
The installation is made up of lines of stainless steel pipes standing on black granite, positioned to exaggerate 'times long past and forever future'. At the end is a small stone structure for sitting and reflecting, providing 'a powerful moment of timeless memory'.
Travis Price

FOOTPRINTS

Lough Lannagh Sculpture Trail, Castlebar

Two of several pieces on the walking circuit around the lake.

Elaine Griffin

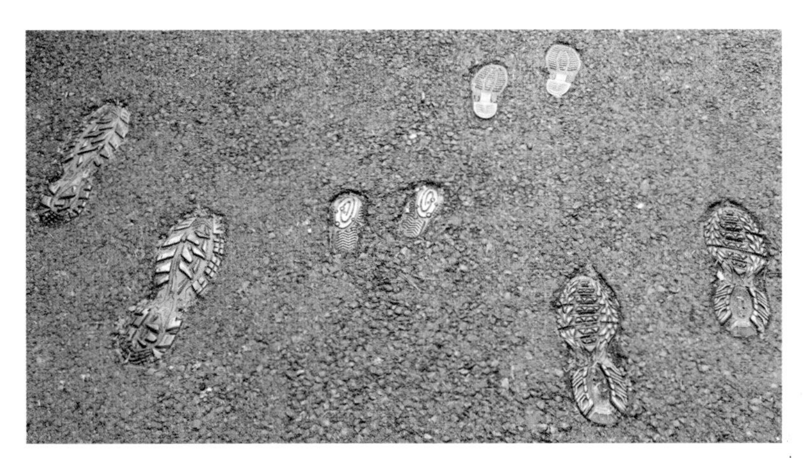

EUROPEAN UNITY

Thomas Street, Castlebar

Limestone and granite; seven standing stones aligned on a sloping site, leading down to a stone tabletop with a dove carved on the surface.

Fred Conlon

THE HOARD AND THE SWORD
Museum of Country Life, Turlough Park
Gary Duffy

WILLOW HORSE
Museum of Country Life,
Turlough Park, Castlebar
Paul O'Driscoll

'98 REMEMBERED
Market Square, Castlebar
Bronze and stainless steel, the pikes are an evocation of the 1798 Rebellion, in particular the episode known as 'the Races of Castlebar'. The doves refer to reconciliation after conflict.
Colm Brennan

UNTITLED
Fire Station, Convent Road, Claremorris
Donegal granite.
Kieran Melody

1916 MEMORIAL
Town Square, Claremorris
In 1966 the town commissioned Edward Delaney, a native of the town, to sculpt a commemorative piece for the 50th anniversary of the 1916 Rising. The installation was blown down in a storm the following year and its remains stood there until Des Prendergast, a member of the commemoration committee, designed a replacement to cover the original work. This was finally unveiled in 1986.

THE QUIET MAN
Cong
Commemorating the filming of John Ford's famous movie in the area in 1951, featuring John Wayne and Maureen O'Hara.
Mark Rode

FLAME
Fire Station, Ballagh Street, Charlestown
Red vertical steel piece, its hollow exterior conceals a light inside.
Marion O'Donnell

FIGURE OF A MAN
Crosspatrick graveyard, Killala
Granite statue marking the grave of sculptor Thomas Mulloy. Local legend has it that Mulloy left an award in his will for the person who closes the undone button of his waistcoat!
Thomas Mulloy

INDEPENDENCE MEMORIAL
N17 at Kilkelly, near Knock Airport
Bronze figure of a man holding a rifle close to his body while climbing a rock incline.
Yann Renard Goulet

MISE RAFTEIRÍ AN FILE
Kiltimagh town centre
The famous Irish-language poet and fiddle-player, blinded by smallpox as a child, was born in the town in 1779.
Sally McKenna

FROM FAMINE FIELDS TO JET STREAMS
Knock Airport
Memorial to former Knock parish priest Monsignor James Horan. He is most widely known for his work on the basilica and for his successful campaign for an airport near Knock. He faced opposition from those who felt that the notion of an airport on a 'foggy boggy site' was unrealistic. It was originally known as Horan International but is now officially Ireland West Airport.
Barry Linnane

WATER FOUNTAINS
Knock Shrine
Two of a collection of images at the water fountains on the grounds.
Imogen Stuart

THREE SAINTS
Beside the Cathedral, Knock Shrine
St Kevin, whose legend relates that he stood still in meditation for so long that birds would nest in his hands; St Patrick, Ireland's patron saint, shown in a Celtic goatskin cloak, with braided hair and beard and with shamrock in hand, as he crushes the snake with his staff; and St Brendan the Navigator, believed to be one of the earliest explorers to reach North America.
Timothy Schmalz

TITANIC MEMORIAL

Addergoole, Laherdane

This village suffered a great loss of life when the *Titanic* sank: of the fourteen men and women who left the area on the ship, eleven died.

Mark Rode

MICHAEL DAVITT

Straide

Bronze and limestone. A significant figure in Irish history, Davitt joined the Fenians in 1865, was arrested for arms-smuggling, was jailed in England for seven years and played a leading role in the Land War of the 1880s.

Rory Breslin

COFFIN SHIP
Murrisk
On a beautiful summer evening the National Famine Memorial is a sobering reminder of the tragedy of the Famine. A bronze ship with skeletons clinging to the rigging, made more poignant by the fact that it is in a tranquil small park with a backdrop of beautiful Clew Bay.
John Behan

SPIRIT OF PLACE—PROCESSION OF SOULS
Famine and Paupers' Graveyard, Swinford
Dedicated to victims of the Great Famine.
Travis Price

CLASPED HANDS

Castlebar Road, Swinford

Commemorating the work of the Sisters of Mercy.

John O'Malley

THE SENTINEL

Town centre, Westport

Bronze and stainless steel angel on a horse, standing on an elevated stone plinth overlooking the town. Commissioned by Westport Town Council in 2013 to celebrate the town's receipt of *The Irish Times* Best Place to Live in Ireland award.

Ronan Halpin

Roscommon

JOSIE
Ballyfarnan
Bronze and Kilkenny limestone piece of the great Irish traditional musician Josie McDermott.
Cathy Carman

FR EDWARD FLANAGAN
Ballymoe
A tribute to the priest who set up Boys' Town in Omaha, Nebraska, on 12 December 1917. He became an acknowledged expert in childcare.
Fred Hoppe

FIVE MOSAIC PANELS
Ballyleague

This wall is all that remains of a children's paddling pool that existed here for over seven decades.

Patsy Preston, Therese and Debbie Tierney, with students of Lanesborough Community College and the Ballyboro Scouts and Venturers

BRANCHES OF UNITY
Cootehall

Forged by members of the Irish Artist Blacksmiths Association to commemorate Shivnans' Forge and the tradition of blacksmithing in the village.

IABA Blacksmiths

WAR OF INDEPENDENCE MEMORIAL
Shankill Cross, Elphin

The names of 40 Roscommon people who died during the War of Independence are on a roll of honour beside this very large stone memorial.

Gary Trimble

LT. GEN. DERMOT EARLEY
Gortnaganny
A tribute to the great Roscommon footballer and chief of staff of the Defence Forces.
Seamus Connolly

GARDA MEMORIAL
Aghaderry, Loughglynn, Ballaghaderreen
In memory of Henry Byrne and John Morley, who were shot following a bank robbery in July 1980.
Michael Carney

GATEWAY OF THE POTATO
Athlone Road, Knockcroghery
Sandstone from Scotland, limestone from the Isle of Portland and blue/grey chippings from nearby Lecarrow Quarry. The piece tells a story of the potato in shape, incised drawings and writing in stone, from its beginnings in South America to Europe.
Nigel Mullan

GALLOWGLASS WARRIOR
N5 Ballaghaderreen Bypass

A gallowglass warrior with his longsword, helmet and armour, which was typically chainmail over a thick coat of linen. The gallowglass was a type of élite mercenary warrior who originated in Scotland.

Clare Bigger

AN CRAOIBHÍN AOIBHINN
Douglas Hyde Interpretative Centre, Frenchpark, Ballaghaderreen

Statue of Douglas Hyde, first president of Ireland, near his home, Ratra House. He is buried in the nearby cemetery with other members of the Hyde family.

Barry Linnane

KEADUE

Brendan Collum

PORTRAIT OF THE SERVICE

Fire Station, Roscommon

Six steel uprights based on information collected by the artist on all incidents reported to Roscommon Fire Service in 2005–7, grouped into categories.

Pamela Wells

FAMINE MEMORIAL

County Memorial Garden, Golf Links Road, Roscommon Town

Maurice Harron and Elizabeth McLaughlin

SURFBOARDER
Village name sign, Tarmonbarry
Kevin Casey

Sligo

US CIVIL WAR MEMORIAL
Ballymote
In memory of Irish Famine emigrants and those of Irish heritage who fought in the American Civil War. At least 200,000 Irishmen served in the armies of both the North and the South.
New York sculptor of Sligo heritage, name unknown to the author

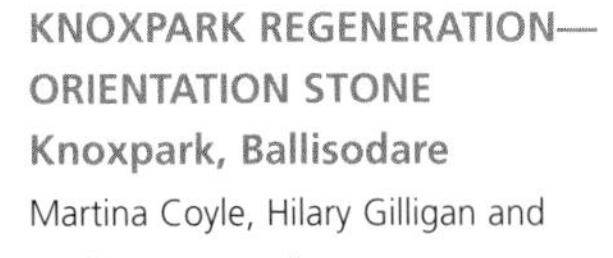

KNOXPARK REGENERATION—ORIENTATION STONE
Knoxpark, Ballisodare
Martina Coyle, Hilary Gilligan and Pauline O'Connell

MICHAEL CORCORAN
Ballymote
Corcoran, who was born in Carrowkeel, was colonel of the 69th New York Militia, 'the Irish Brigade', in the Civil War, and led the regiment in the First Battle of Bull Run. He was also the founder of the Fenian Brotherhood in America. Underneath the monument is a piece of steel from the World Trade Centre, donated by the family of Michael Lynch, who died in New York's 9/11 attack. Lynch's family are from Sligo.
Philip Flanagan

BROTHER WALFRID
The Park, Ballymote
Bronze on limestone plinth of Andrew Kerins, Brother Walfrid, who was born in Ballymote and founded Celtic Football Club in Glasgow.
Mark Rode

HANDS ON SLASH GLASS
Racecourse View, Cranmore
Glass and steel, commissioned by Cluaid Housing Association.
Christine Mackay

LEAF SEATS
Riparian River Walk, Coolaney
Giant bronze leaves, cast using Bronze Age casting methods and representing the leaves of trees growing nearby. They are a development of the same theme in an earlier work—'Woodlands'—in Clonakilty.
Alex Pentek

TIME OF DAY

Easkey

Celebrating the bicycle as a mode of transport and recalling a time when people had time to stop and chat.

Cillian Rogers

12 BURIAL SLABS

Carrowntemple, Gorteen

Replicas of Early Christian burial slabs at the burial ground in Carrowntemple, from where five of the originals were taken in 1984. A priest later admitted removing them in order to preserve them.

Cillian Rogers

SERPENT

Coláiste Iascaigh, Easkey

Colourful mosaic snake.

Áine Kelly and Valli Schafer, with students

HARMONY

Coleman Music Centre, Gurteen

Two pieces connected by colour and space. A key part of the design was the outer layer with its negative spaces and the interwoven pattern which casts shadows and creates movement on the internal instrument, appearing both abstract and figurative.

Aoife McCarrick

DAONNACHT

St Angela's College, Lough Gill

White stone composite over a stainless steel armature. The college commissioned this piece to commemorate its 60th anniversary in 2013.

Bettina Seitz

SUNDIAL AND TIME CAPSULE

Mullaghmore

Memorial to deceased people of the area.

Brendan McGloinn

COMING HOME

Markree Castle Home Farm

Three pieces at a water feature, two on the avenue from the river and one sitting with a bowl in the courtyard: marble composite figures inspired by the location of Markree Castle farm—bringing back produce to the courtyard from fields and river.

Bettina Seitz

THE BULL PILLAR
Riverstown
Martha Quinn

COUNTESS MARKIEVICZ
Rathcormack
Constance Markievicz fought in the 1916 Easter Rising, received a death sentence which was commuted on account of her sex, was the first woman member of the British House of Commons (though she did not take her seat) and the second woman in the world to hold a cabinet position—Minister for Labour in Dublin. My favourite quotation of hers: 'Dress suitably in short skirts and strong boots, leave your jewels and gold wands in the bank, and buy a revolver'.
John Coll

SALMON OF KNOWLEDGE
Institute of Technology, Ash Lane, Sligo
Steel on stone plinth.
Brian Halpin

CONVERSATIONS

Nazareth House Nursing Home, Church Hill, Sligo

Four white figures in stone composite over stainless steel armatures, celebrating the opening of the new nursing home in 2008. The theme is conversation, reflected in the positioning of the figures: at the building's entrance and in the courtyard outside the café.

Bettina Seitz

PATHWAY

Nazareth House Nursing Home, Church Hill, Sligo

Twelve ceramic pieces, the concept of which is the cycle of life broken down into four headings: spring, summer, autumn and winter.

Catherine Fanning and Brigitta Varadi

THE FAMINE FAMILY
Fish Quay, Sligo

Bronze memorial to mark the 150th anniversary of Black '47, showing a Famine family comforting each other before emigration.

Niall Bruton

DEFENCE FORCES MEMORIAL
Doorly Park, Sligo

In memory of Defence Forces personnel from the Sligo area who died on peace-keeping duties overseas: Dermot McLoughlin, Mannix Armstrong and Thomas Walsh.

Jackie McKenna and Seamus Dunbar

W.B. YEATS
Stephen Street, Sligo
Bronze of one of the twentieth century's greatest poets, on a cobbled stone plinth.
Rowan Gillespie

Leinster

Carlow

OLD LADY BURNING LEAVES
Tullow Street, Carlow
Reconstituted granite figure based on a painting by nineteenth-century Carlow-born painter Frank O'Meara.
Patrick Randall

TEMPLECRONEY STONE
The Quay, Graigue, Carlow
Limestone sculpture map of Carlow.
Michelle Byrne

NANO NAGLE
Scoil Mhuire gan Smál, Green Lane, Carlow
Born to a wealthy Catholic family in Mallow, Co. Cork, Nano Nagle, the founder of the Presentation Order of nuns, devoted her life to the education of poor children. By day she visited her schools and at night she helped the poor of Cork city, becoming known as 'the Lady of the Lantern'.
Annette McCormack

VIGILANCE
Fire Station, Carlow
Bronze bell, complete with its Christmas lights and decoration!
Niall O'Neill

GENERATIONS
Teagasc Agriculture Advisory Centre, Oak Park, Carlow
Fabricated bronze.
Cathy Carman

BOXING HARES
The Lord Bagenal, Leighlinbridge
Wire-mesh piece of movement and energy.
Gwen Wilkinson

Dublin

DEARCAN NA nDAOINE / THE PEOPLE'S ACORN

Áras an Uachtaráin

This sculpture commemorates the momentous events of 1916. Using thousands of collected pencils, the bronze acorn is modelled from the seed of our national tree, the native sessile oak. A seed is like a time capsule that carries its own history; the time capsule within this piece houses the many memories and wishes written across two generational groups, collected by the sculptor in collaboration with poet Enda Wyley. Unveiled by President Michael D. Higgins on 14 December 2017.

Rachel Joynt

THE PLOUGH AND THE STARS

Áras an Uachtaráin

Commemorating the 1913 Lockout, when impoverished Dublin workers went on strike in August 1913 for better conditions and the right to join a trade union. They were locked out by the employers from then until spring 1914 in order to starve them back to work. The plough was gifted by Irish ploughing champion Gerry King.

John Behan

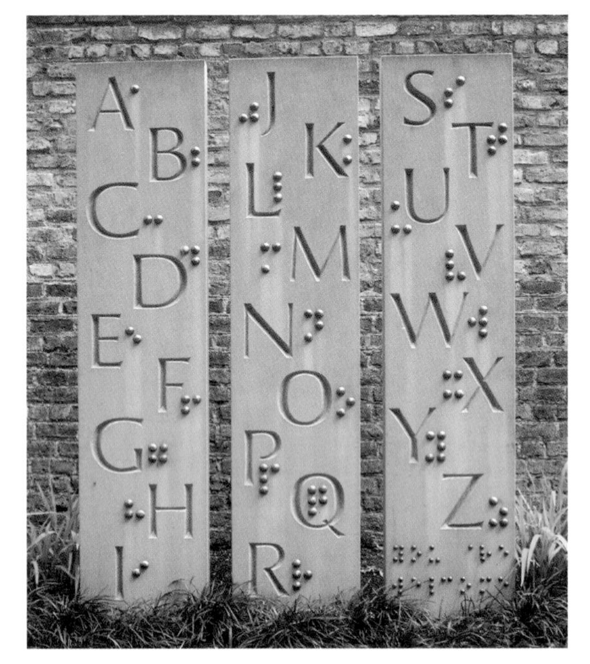

THE BRAILLE ALPHABET
Sensory Garden, Áras an Uachtaráin
Three panels covering the senses of sight and touch: the alphabet letters are V-cut into the stone and beside each letter is the Braille equivalent in bronze.
Richie Healy

BLUEBELLS
Sensory Garden, Áras an Uachtaráin
Interactive cast-bronze piece: seven bluebells that hang at various heights and make different ringing sounds.
Richie Healy

TASTE
Sensory Garden, Áras an Uachtaráin
The glass strawberry on a steel fork appears to be plunging through the wall. It suggests someone snatching the fruit from the garden behind the wall, or tempting a passer-by with the strawberry.
Róisín de Buitléar

GATEWAY
Main Entrance, Dublin City University, Glasnevin
54 pillars of accoya glulam wood.
ZAP Architecture

THE ROSE BOWL
Main Mall, Dublin City University, Glasnevin
Representing 32-year-old Rose Atieno, who died of AIDS in Kenya in 2003. She was the sixteen-millionth person to die of the disease in Sub-Saharan Africa, and the forty-millionth worldwide. The cast-bronze piece commemorates Rose and all who lost their lives to AIDS.
Sandra Bell

Two images of Luke Kelly, the legendary folk singer, musician and founder member of *The Dubliners* folk group, were unveiled on both sides of the Liffey on 30 January 2019, the 35th anniversary of his death.

South King Street
Cast-bronze life-size image of the distinctive figure of Luke in an area associated with him as a musician and Dublin figure.
John Coll

Sherriff Street
Marble and metal piece mounted on a concrete plinth along the Royal Canal in the north inner city docklands area near the singer's birthplace.
Vera Klute

COUNT JOHN McCORMACK

Iveagh Gardens

Bronze figure of the world-famous tenor, who was born in Athlone in 1884. His voice quality and charisma made him the most successful concert performer of the early twentieth century.

Elizabeth O'Kane

MAGNUS MODUS

National Gallery of Ireland, Merrion Square

Olive ash, white oil finish and Kilkenny limestone base. An exception to my outdoor sculpture rule, but I include this iconic piece to commemorate the reopening of the beautifully refurbished National Gallery of Ireland in 2017.

Joseph Walsh

RED SQUIRREL

George's Quay

Car parts, bicycle wheels, plastic barriers and other waste materials make up this piece.

Artur Bordalo

RIVER RAT
Erne Street Upper
At the pedestrian tunnel of the railway bridge the rat, in Kilkenny limestone, commemorates the maritime history of the docklands area. The life-size piece is sitting at ground level and is the only cute rat I have ever seen!
Jason Ellis

MICHAEL CUSACK
Croke Park
In 1884 Cusack and Maurice Davin founded the Gaelic Athletic Association at a meeting in Hayes Hotel in Thurles, Co. Tipperary. Davin was elected president and Cusack became its first secretary.
Paul Ferriter

PLANE TREE
Incorporated Orthopaedic Hospital of Ireland, Castle Avenue, Clontarf
Sheet-bronze tree; Hippocrates taught his pupils the art of medicine under a plane tree in Kos.
Elizabeth O'Kane

HAND OF HOPE
Donore Avenue
In memory of all those who died as a result of addiction.
Leonardo Benasalvas

EASTER ISLAND *MOAI*
Clontarf seafront
Replica of an ancient Easter Island head or *moai*, sculpted in Chile of volcanic stone from Easter Island and presented to the City of Dublin by the Deputy Foreign Minister on behalf of the government of Chile.
Alejandro Pakarati

FREEWHEELING CHAMP
Main Street, Dundrum
In honour of Stephen Roche, the famous cyclist, who is a native of Dundrum. The piece was commissioned by the bicycle shopkeeper in Dundrum who supplied parts to the young Roche. The bronze design represents bicycle gears and the lettered granite circle the movement of the wheels.
Cliodna Cussen

RIALTO
Rialto roundabout
Between the Grand Canal and what was the working canal for the Guinness Brewery, a bronze piece depicting a figure enveloped by two fish. Commissioned by the people of Rialto.
Sandra Bell

RICHARD CROSBIE
Ranelagh Gardens
On 19 January 1785 Crosbie launched his hydrogen balloon from Ranelagh Gardens and made a short flight to Clontarf.
Rory Breslin

DEARTHÁIREACHA / BROTHERS

Pearse Museum, St Enda's, Rathfarnham

The remains of a century-old Californian redwood have been transformed into a piece commemorating the Pearse brothers, who were executed for their part in the 1916 Easter Rising.

Liam O'Neill

ANNE DEVLIN

Rathfarnham Village

After her family's support for the 1798 Rebellion, Anne moved into Robert Emmet's house to help with his plans for an uprising in Dublin in 1803—a rising that collapsed. She was afterwards arrested and tortured in an attempt to extract information on Emmet's whereabouts. She refused to speak but he was nevertheless found and executed. She later married, had three children and died in 1861.

Clodagh Emoe

MARLAY PARK

SOLITARY FIGURE

From one side of the figure the sun reflects the stainless steel shine and it appears to be a two-dimensional image from the future; from the other side the cut-out shape is a dark, menacing shadow emerging from the trees.

Cathy Carman

NECROMANCY

Constructed from strips of thick steel plate, the sections are cut, shaped and welded together to form the features of a figure with its arm outstretched and directed towards a glaring head emerging from the grass a couple of metres away.

Vincent Brown

ECLIPSE

Cylindrical limestone piece standing upright, appearing to defy gravity by not rolling over from the weight of the piece attached to its side.

Eileen MacDonagh

DREAMING ABOUT THE CELESTIAL MOUNTAIN

Concrete and earthworks piece about journeys that will never take place except in the imagination. The path to the summit forms a labyrinth, and steps are inscribed with a poem describing the preparations for a successful journey.

Agnes Conway

LOVE ALL
Templeogue Village
Cast-bronze revolving globe that seems like a tennis ball but is actually like a miniature world, depicting a river, bridges, houses and mountains.
Rachel Joynt

MISNEACH
Trinity Comprehensive School, Main Street, Ballymun
Bronze, celebrating the tradition of young people riding horses bareback around Dublin. This horse is a copy of the one on the Gough memorial in Phoenix Park that was blown up in 1957 and which Sir Humphrey Wakefield, a descendant of Gough, restored and erected at his home at Chillingham Castle, Northumberland. The rider is modelled on a 3D laser scan taken of a local teenager, Toni Marie Shields.
John Byrne

ANOTHER SPHERE
Balcurris Park, Ballymun
The subjects reflected on the surfaces of the two spheres are filmed on CCTV and transmitted to a central broadcasting point. The two hemispheres only come together to form a full circle on the plasma screen. Playing with the idea of surveillance in a positive way, the piece allows passers-by to be included as part of the work.
Kevin Atherton

MAIDE DOLCÁIN / STAFF OF DOLCAN
Garda Station, Clondalkin
The name Clondalkin, *Cluain Dolcáin* ('Dolcan's meadow'), suggests that this person may have been a chieftain, and this represents his ceremonial staff.
Colm Brennan

FLOWERS
Hansfield Educate Together School, Barnwell Road, Blanchardstown
Wild Metal

TALLAGHT X
Library Square, Tallaght
Four rectangular stainless steel pillars that tilt and lean against each other. The top half of each one is striped with parallel polished mirror-like lines that reflect the square around the installation.
Eileen MacDonagh

GEATA NA NEALAÍ / SWANGATE

Main Street, Donabate

Bronze piece consisting of two inverted L-shapes joined to form an arch or gateway. Low-relief images of two swans flying over water occupy the outside surfaces, celebrating the dozens of swans that nest around the local estuary, as well as marking the swan's special place in Irish mythology.

Niall O'Neill

DRAGON FAMILY

St George's National School, Naul Road, Balbriggan

Stainless steel with powder-coated dragons.

Jim Collins

TREE OF LIFE

St Joseph's Secondary School, Convent Lane, Rush

Stainless steel oak tree celebrating the golden jubilee of the school. Each leaf represents a year in the school's life and each bird represents a decade of the school's existence. There are 50 ceramic hand impressions of students and staff from the past 50 years, fired and glazed by Frances Brosnan, and also silhouettes of a boy and girl, representing the co-educational nature of the school.

Paul Flynn

CRÓNÁN NA GLAISE MÓIRE

Brackenstown

Tradition has it that Crónán was killed by the Vikings—hence the longship in the background.

Séighean Ó Draoi

THE RAVEN

Dublin Road Roundabout, Lusk

The raven is the symbol of Fingal.

Bríd Ní Rínn

EMBRACING SEALS
Main Street, Skerries
Paul D'Arcy

SEA POLE MEMORIAL
Skerries
Restoration of an old sea rescue pole as a memorial commemorating those lost in the seas around Skerries and Loughshinny.
Shane Holland

SEAMUS ENNIS
The renowned uilleann piper, who died in 1982, also worked for the Irish Folklore Commission as a collector of Irish traditional music and song. He is widely regarded as one of the greatest uilleann pipers of all time and was partly responsible for the revival of the instrument during the twentieth century.
Vincent Brown

CARVED TREE

St Anne's Park, Bull Island

The artist sculpted a variety of birds, animals and sea creatures on the stump of a Monterey cypress tree which had been cut down for health and safety reasons.

Tommy Craggs

APPLES AND ATOMS

School of Physics, Trinity College

Commemorating the 80th anniversary of the 1932 experiment when Ernest Walton and John Crockford split the atom. For their pioneering work the men were jointly awarded the Nobel Prize for Physics in 1951.

Eilis O'Connell

CHAC MOOL

Near Lincoln Gate, Trinity College

'Chac mool', the name of the greatest Mayan warrior, is the name given to a type of ancient Mesoamerican sculpture found in Central Mexico, depicting a reclining figure resting on its elbows with its legs bent upwards. The spray-painted mild steel piece was donated to the college by the Mexican artist; its unveiling in 2015 marked 40 years of Irish–Mexican diplomatic relations.

Sebastian

HOMELESS JESUS

Christ Church Cathedral

Designed to raise awareness of homelessness, this is a bronze park bench with a Christ figure covered by a blanket lying on it, recognisable only by the holes in his feet.

Timothy Schmalz

HANDEL

Fishamble Street

Copper and bronze statue of the composer near the spot where his *Messiah* was first performed in 1742.

Laurent Mellet

WHO MADE THE WORLD?

Beside the Dodder, Ballsbridge

People holding up the globe while recovering from the infamous March 2018 snowstorm known as 'the Beast from the East'.

Cliodna Cussen

SALVADOR MEMORIAL BELL

Jesuit House, Milltown Park

Erected by the Irish Jesuits and the Irish El Salvador Support Committee in memory of the thousands killed in the struggle, referred to as '*la lucha*', for justice in El Salvador. The victims of *la lucha* who are commemorated in this memorial include Archbishop Oscar Romero, who was assassinated in San Salvador in 1980, and the six Jesuits and a mother and daughter killed at the Jesuit University of Central America in San Salvador in 1989.

Michael Burke

UNIVERSITY COLLEGE DUBLIN

FIGUREHEAD

Roebuck Student Residence

Kilkenny limestone, at one of the gateways into Belfield campus. The combined weight of the four blocks is twenty tons, and it is one of the tallest free-standing stone sculptures in the country.

Jason Ellis

BLACK TULIP

Science Centre, beside the lake

RKD Architects, who designed the Science Centre, donated this piece to UCD to commemorate the 100th anniversary of RKD.

Éamonn Ceannt

UNIVERSITY COLLEGE DUBLIN

FORME IN MUTAZIONE
Beside the lake
Inox steel, donated by the late Italian ambassador to Ireland, Dr Francesco Carlo Gentile.
Giorgio Zennaro

IPHIGENIA
Main Restaurant
Iphigenia, the daughter of Agamemnon, was sacrificed to enable the Greek fleet to sail for the siege of Troy.
Thomas Glendon

PORTAL
Sutherland School of Law
Bronze.
Catherine Green

JUDGEMENT
Sutherland School of Law
Bronze.
Rowan Gillespie

CUT-OUT PEOPLE
Blackrock Park
Figures stand on a plinth, with painted patterns representing the shadows from the sun. The design is two- and three-dimensional.
Dan McCarthy

DR MICHAEL SMURFIT
UCD Smurfit Graduate Business School, Carysford Avenue, Blackrock
The businessman joined his father's company, Jefferson Smurfit & Sons, in 1955 and retired in 2002.
John Coll

BIRD-BATH
Rochestown Gardens,
off Rochestown Avenue
The tapering granite pillar is carved with woodland motifs and resembles a bird-bath.
Cliodna Cussen

TOWER TO THE HOBBLERS

Dún Laoghaire Pier

A tower of 64 life-size cast-bronze life-jackets commemorating the deaths of numerous hobblers. These were men who guided vessels into the port and assisted mooring right up to the 1930s.

Fiona Mulholland

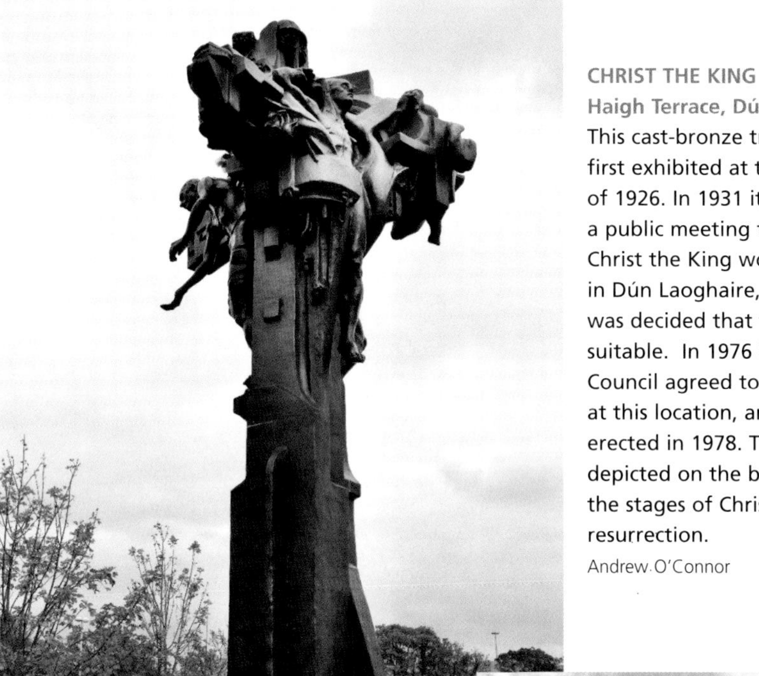

CHRIST THE KING

Haigh Terrace, Dún Laoghaire

This cast-bronze triple cross was first exhibited at the Paris Salon of 1926. In 1931 it was agreed at a public meeting that a statue of Christ the King would be erected in Dún Laoghaire, and in 1949 it was decided that this one was suitable. In 1976 Dún Laoghaire Council agreed to the siting of it at this location, and it was erected in 1978. The three scenes depicted on the bronze pillar are the stages of Christ's death and resurrection.

Andrew O'Connor

SERPENTINE SEAT

Ferry Terminal, Dún Laoghaire

Seating with copper and indigo hand-painted mosaics inlaid with glass and steel features.

Orla Kaminska

In the background is 'Gaoth na Sáile' by Éamonn O'Doherty.

1916 COMMEMORATIVE SCULPTURE

Deansgrange Cemetery

Limestone with granite base.

Thomas Glendon

UNTITLED
Entrance to Cromlech Fields, Killiney Hill Road
Standing at the entrance to the housing estate, the two large pieces of granite are reminiscent of a dolmen acting as a gateway to the estate, with a bronze section connecting them.
Maurice MacDonagh

MOTHER AND CHILD
Ballinclea Heights family park
Mounted on a granite plinth, this is an abstract bronze form depicting a mother and child embracing. The inspiration for the piece comes from the flower of a plant known as 'lords and ladies'.
Michael Whelan

SPEND A PENNY?
Exterior of a public toilet, Killiney beach carpark
These relief bronze panels are bathroom symbols. The sculptor used Celtic figures set against the background of the Dublin mountains.
Cathy MacAleavey

THEATRE
Cabinteely Park
This very dramatic installation in the grounds of Cabinteely House is cast in granite. The performers—the masks on white pillars—represent human vices such as malice, greed and violence, while the audience holds itself apart from them.
Agnes Conway

ELEMENTS

Ravenscourt Business Park, Sandyford

Series of installations in the business park, in terrazzo with glass aggregate/stainless steel. Commissioned by Brian O'Halloran Architects.

Niall Walsh

PARK WEST

SPIRAL WALL

Park West main entrance, Nangor Road

Acting as a welcoming piece, this mosaic spiral wall is a representation of the Park West logo: five bronze circles with internal fibre-optic lights stand in relief from the wall. The lettering of Park West is also internally lit.

Ronan Halpin

THE BASTARD SON OF SISYPHUS

Yeats Way

Bronze figure and limestone megaliths above a stepped waterfall with a bronze ball below. Derived from the Greek myth of Sisyphus, who was punished for his arrogance by being condemned by the gods to push a large rock uphill and watch it roll back down again for all eternity.

Orla de Brí

WAVE

Guinness Reservoir, Yeats Way

A twisting, 37m-tall spiral; the tip can sway up to 6m in the wind and return to its central position by way of a ten-ton lead counterweight. Carbon fibre, steel frame with a granite and marble surround, it is inspired by Islamic calligraphy and saplings blowing in the wind.

Angela Conner

DANCING CRANES

Block 9, Beckett Way

Two bronze cranes perform a dramatic dance after completing their migratory journey.

Lloyd Le Blanc

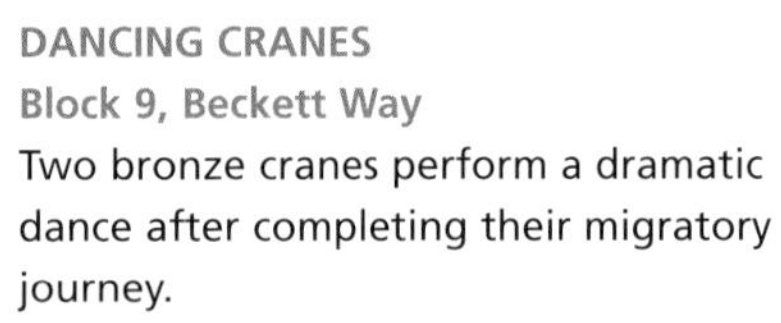

MEETING

Block 7, Beckett Way

This polished aluminium site-specific installation represents people meeting to do business.

Patrick Loughran

ST KILIAN
St Kilian's German School,
Roebuck Road
Leitrim sandstone, carved by
McKeon Stone.
Cathy Carman

FISH
Howth
Bronze.
Tanya Nyegaard

HERON
Howth
Bronze.
Alva Gallagher
Both pieces the property of the late
Feargal Quinn and Denise Quinn.

Kildare

BRIGID OF KILDARE
Scoil Bhríde, Athgarvan
The large-scale steel piece on the school grounds, representing an inspirational woman of fifth-century Ireland, is rich in symbolism and mythology.
Lynn Kirkham

ERNEST SHACKLETON
Emily Square, Athy
Alexandra Shackleton at the unveiling of the statue of her grandfather. The great Antarctic explorer is facing south, where he spent many years of his life and where he now lies in South Georgia among the whalers who played such a significant role in his epic trek across the island with Tom Crean and Frank Worsley.
Mark Richards

JOURNEYING TOGETHER
Ballylinan National School, Athy
Representation of a murmuration of birds. The theme of the piece is continued on the back wall of the school and inside the entrance. I was told that some of the children salute the indoor bird when they pass by!
Mark Ryan and Maree Hensey

FAMINE FAMILY
St Vincent's Hospital,
Woodstock Street, Athy
Carved from 4,000-year-old black oak, the figures of father, mother and child reflect the human tragedy of the Irish people.
James McKenna

SYNTHESIS
Ballitore
Corten steel and stainless steel.
Ned Jackson Smyth

THE BALLITORE TRUNK
Main Street, Ballitore
Beaten copper-sheet piece based on the shape of an ancient travelling trunk used in the era of the Bianconi coaches that passed through the village, with each panel commemorating local people and events. The piece was the outcome of workshops with the Griese Living History Group, which is part of the Ballitore Youth Theatre Group.
Fifi Smith

THE GALLOP

Ballymany Roundabout, Kildare

Tubular steel installation inspired by the railing of the Curragh racetrack. Four stages of the gallop are frozen and outlined by the railing. As passers-by move around the roundabout, the piece creates a sense of the movement of running horses.

Paul Finch

NAMESTONES

Liffey Court, Ballymore Eustace

Three houses as an add-on to an older estate, so the artist carved a triskele—three spirals—on the front. The reverse has patterns similar to a La Tène-style carving on the Turoe Stone.

Aileen-Anne Barrington

ARCH
Main Street, Ballymore Eustace
Imogen Stuart

UNTITLED
National School, Main Street, Caragh
The artists worked with the schoolchildren to evolve the form, scale and medium of the sculpture. Involving the children in the work brought a sense of ownership, and the resulting piece has become an integral part of the school.
Mark Ryan and Maree Hensey

HOMEWARD
M9 at Ballymount
A representation of a window with a pitcher of bluebells on the sill.
Éamonn O'Doherty

ARTHUR GUINNESS

Town centre, Celbridge

The founder of the Guinness Brewery was born in the town in 1725 and lived there until he moved to James's Street in Dublin in 1759, where Guinness is still brewed today.

Jarlath Daly

VINTAGE CROP

Curragh Racecourse

Owned by Michael Smurfit and trained by Dermot Weld, this horse competed in flat racing in Ireland, England and Australia in 1992–5, with wins in the Cesarewitch Handicap, the Curragh Cup, the Irish St Leger and the Melbourne Cup.

Emma MacDermott

NIJINSKY

Curragh Racecourse

An outstanding Canadian-bred Irish-trained racehorse with major victories in 1969–70. Among his wins were the 2000 Guineas, the Epsom Derby, the Irish Derby, and the King George VI and Queen Elizabeth Stakes. He was retired to stud in 1970 and a film, *A horse called Nijinsky*, was made about his racing career. Lester Piggott said that he was one of the two best horses he ever rode.

Emma MacDermott

THE TWIN TOWERS

Donadea Forest Park

The model of the twin tower blocks carries the names of all the men and women of the New York Fire Department, police officers and Port Authority officials who died in the 9/11 attacks. It especially honours the memory of fireman Seán Tallon, whose father came from Donadea.

Brian Swan

PEGASUS
K Club, Straffan
Life-sized bronze triptych of Pegasus, the winged horse of Greek mythology, each piece weighing half a ton.
Conor Fallon

UNTITLED
Scoil Uí Riada, Kilcock
A large-scale acoustic sound sculpture loosely based on the funnelled form of an ancient Celtic torc. As an acoustic receiver and amplifier, the work symbolises the important role of the school as a vehicle of communication and expression.
Alex Pentek

THE MAGICIAN
Main Street, Kilcullen
Black Indian granite piece commissioned to celebrate the achievement of Paddy Nugent, founder of the Kilcullen Development Association, which brought industry and social housing to the town. The intaglio image on the piece is the face of Paddy Nugent himself, taken from a plaster cast.
Noel Scullion

INVISIBLE PRESENCE
Cross and Passion School, Kilcullen
Marking the presence of the nuns at the college and the end of their tenure there—their invisible presence will remain. The face on the intaglio image is that of Sr Carmel, one of the last nuns to leave.
Noel Scullion

TROUT AND FLY
Town centre, Kilcullen
The trout is the most common fish in the River Liffey, which flows through the town. The design is based on the art style of the indigenous people of the north-west coast of the United States.
Kieran Behan

BRIGID
St Brigid's Well, between Kildare and the National Stud
Figure of St Brigid with staff and flame.
Annette McCormack

HEART OF OAK
St Brigid's Square, Kildare
Galway granite and Wicklow granite. The acorn symbolises Cill Dara as a piece split in half, with a germinating acorn revealed on the inside, like a fossil in a positive and negative. This middle split aligns with the midday sun. Commissioned by Irish Business Against Litter in 2017.
Noel Scullion

ST BRIGID AND CHILDREN
St Brigid's National School, Kill
The saint leads pupils into the school, and the silhouette theme is also used on the outside walls. The designs are enlarged reproductions of student ideas for 'school lifecycles'.
Paul Finch

MUSIC FISH

Gaelscoil Uí Fhiaich, Celbridge Road, Maynooth

The symbols are subtle in this welded and fabricated stainless steel piece. The fish has an open mouth and dragon-like teeth, waiting for predators. Over the head a listening device in the form of a periscope watches over the immediate environment, protecting the school's ideals and ethos.

Joe Butler

WAGGLE DANCE

Iontas Building, National University of Ireland, Maynooth

Made from curved plate bronze perforated by holes of various sizes, revealing an internal stainless steel cellular substructure. It represents the creativity and intellectual endeavour of the university through the geometry of the beehive.

Rachel Joynt and Remco de Fouw

CORNUCOPIA

Monread North, Naas

Barry Linnane

JOHN DEVOY

Town centre, Naas

Born in Kill in 1842, Devoy spent some time in the French Foreign Legion, then joined the Fenians when he returned home. After almost five years in prison he went to the US, where he remained active in Clann na Gael for many decades. He returned to Ireland when an old man, died in 1928 and is buried in Glasnevin.

Jarlath Daly

SENTINEL

Buckley's Cross Roundabout, Newbridge

Brush-polished stainless steel stylised abstract figure commemorating both the bicentenary of Newbridge and the tenure of the town council—a sentinel or guard at the entrance to the town, bearing the symbol of Newbridge 200, which was an acknowledgement of passing milestones.

James Hayes

COSANTÓIR / PROTECTOR

The Strand park, Newbridge

Bronze swan.

Annette McCormack

MARKET-PLACE PANELS
George's Street, Newbridge
Bronze relief panels depicting market traders.
Ann Meldon Hugh

PAUSE FOR THOUGHT
Ann Street, Prosperous
Bronze piece of two parents watching over their children at play. The residents were instrumental in getting the piece installed and the children helped Caragh Nurseries with planting and maintenance.
Catherine Greene

GHOST HORSES FROM THE BOG
Nurney Roundabout, M7
Four larger-than-life horse sculptures in bog oak and galvanised steel.
Lynn Kirkham

SPIRIT OF GORDON BENNETT

Timolin

A set of free-standing mild steel silhouettes with matt black polyester powder coating. The 1903 Gordon Bennett Cup was the first international motor race held in Ireland on a closed roads circuit of Laois/Carlow/Kildare. The piece is a silhouette of the winning car crossing the finish line—a Mercedes driven by the three-time land-speed record-breaker, Belgian Camille Jenatzy. He was also the first person to break the 100km per hour barrier. Ironically, he died not at the wheel of a car, as one might expect with such a daredevil, but when he was out hunting with friends. He made animal noises from behind a bush to play a prank on his companions and sounded so authentic that they shot him. The question now is whether that chicken managed to outrun the fox!

Fifi Smith

SEA OF STARS

Irish National Stud, Tully

Bronze sphere featuring the North constellation in January. Inside is a horse with arched neck, looking up at the sky. The artist tells the story of the brilliant eccentric William Hall Walker, who used horoscopes as a breeding aid and had stables with glass ceilings for the horses.

Anthony Scott

HALL WALKER
Irish National Stud, Tully
Colonel William Hall Walker, the founder of the Irish National Stud.
Bob Quinn

DRIFTWOOD MARE AND FOAL
Irish National Stud, Tully
The Indonesian artist says that 'the beauty, courage, grace and movement of a horse are like living, breathing poetry'.
Abdul Ghofur

Kilkenny

EDMUND IGNATIUS RICE
Green Street, Callan
The founder of the Christian Brothers and the Presentation Brothers, who devoted his life to the education of the poor, was born in Callan in 1762.
Peter Grant

MoDOMNOC
N24 near Fiddown
MoDomnoc was an Irish bishop who had been a disciple of St David in Wales. When he returned to Ireland he was followed by swarms of bees, and thus they were introduced to this country. He ended his life as a hermit near Fiddown.
Austin McQuinn

MONKS OF DUISKE

Graiguenamanagh

The Cistercians established Duiske Abbey in 1204. It is believed that there was no settlement of any kind in the area prior to their arrival, though one may have formed outside the abbey walls. With the dissolution of the abbey under Henry VIII, stones and other material from it were used to build the town of Graiguenamanagh. In effect, the monks arrived first and the town was later constructed from the ruins. Early in the nineteenth century the local community refurbished the abbey church, and another major refurbishment was carried out between 1974 and 1984. In 2004, to commemorate the 800th anniversary of the founding of the abbey, the Tidy Towns Committee undertook an ambitious project to place twelve granite sculptures of monks around the town. Amazingly, this was accomplished in four years, and the result is a tribute to their determination. Spread around the town and its environs are monks engaged in a variety of tasks.

THE ABBOT, Main Street

THE STONEMASON, entrance to Fairgreen Park

Below, left to right: THE SCRIBE, High Street; THE BASKET-MAKER, Barrow Bridge; THE SHEEP-SHEARER, New Ross Road, facing the Blackstairs Mountains; THE HARVESTER, bypass at Inistioge Road, gazing at snowy Mount Leinster

Left to right: THE DAIRY WORKER, Borris Road; THE WOODCUTTER, Silaire Wood; THE SALMON FISHER, downriver from Barrow Bridge

Left to right: THE EEL FISHER, upriver from Barrow Bridge; THE GARDENER, Tinnahinch; THE HUNTER, St Mullins Road, Tinnahinch

HURLERS
Canal Square, John's Bridge
Typical scene in the great hurling county.
Barry Wrafter

LOAVES AND FISHES
Kells Priory, Kells
Kevin Fennelly

DUCK MURAL
Mary's Lane, Kilkenny
Colourful mural on a garage door.
Dan Leo

MEMORIAL TO MISSING PERSONS
Kilkenny Castle grounds
Bronze piece depicting the handprints of the relatives of missing persons, commissioned by the JoJo Dullard Memorial Trust.
Ann Mulrooney

PHEASANT MURAL
Under Ossory Bridge, Kilkenny
Dan Leo

BOY MURAL
Under Ossory Bridge, Kilkenny
Mick Minogue

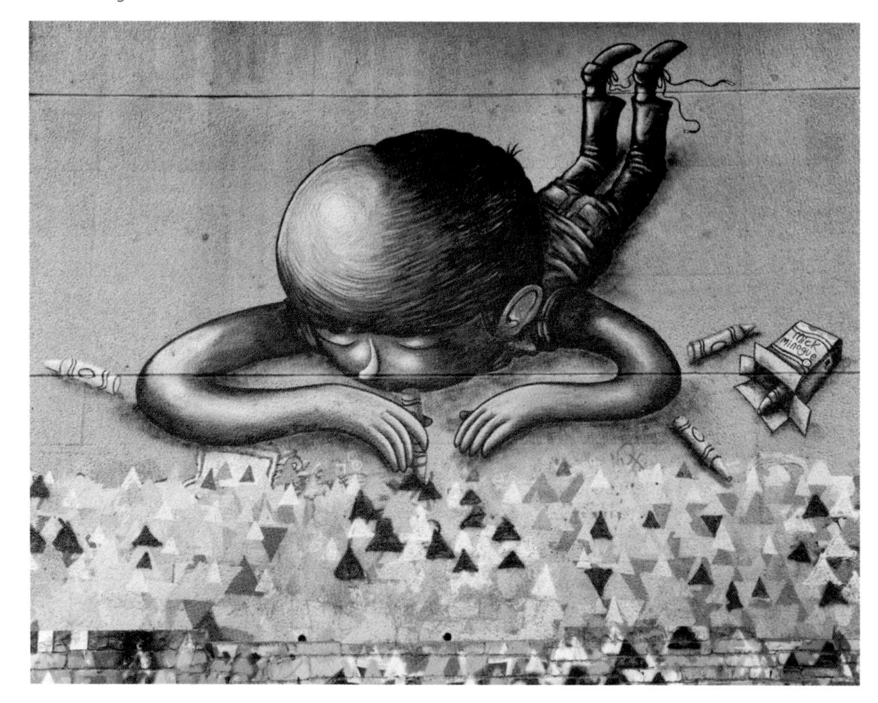

GIANT BLUEBELLS
Hennebry's Cross, Kilkenny/Castlecomer Road
The piece was designed especially for this part of Kilkenny—the nearby Jenkinstown Woods are famous for bluebells.
Wild Metal

OLLIE WALSH
Thomastown
Bronze piece commemorating the famous hurler, who died in 1996. He is usually holding the Kilkenny flag!
Jerry McKenna

GLOBE
Dublin Road roundabout, Urlingford
Globe map of the world. The artist, who constructed this piece in three weeks, wanted to honour the local people who were forced to emigrate during the almost decade-long recession that began in 2008. The four corners of the world are indicated by the corners of the flower-bed at the base of the installation.
Martin Campion

CANTWELL FADA, LONG MAN OF KILFANE
Fourteenth-century Kilfane Church ruin, north of Thomastown
A Norman knight, in relief, whose posture marks him as a Crusader.
Artist's name unknown to the author

HURLER
At Tulla Church, Three Castles
Kilkenny limestone hurler honouring All-Ireland medallists from Three Castles GAA Club.
Ruairí Carroll

Laois

SEVERIANO BALLESTEROS
The Heritage Golf Club, Killenard
Seve, a very popular Spanish golfer who turned professional at the age of sixteen, was a world number one, and was one of the sport's leading figures from the mid-1970s to the 1990s.
Paul Ferriter

FLOW
Clonkeen, Portlaoise Bypass
A Three Castles Kilkenny limestone piece inspired by the aerial view of the River Nore as it meanders through the local landscape, carved by McKeon Stone in Stradbally.
Eileen MacDonagh

DRIFTWOOD DEER
1916 Commemorative Garden, Killenard
Charlie Burke

METAL SCULPTURES

Dunamaise Theatre, Church Street, Portlaoise

Interrelated pieces of low-relief metal sculpture.

John O'Connor

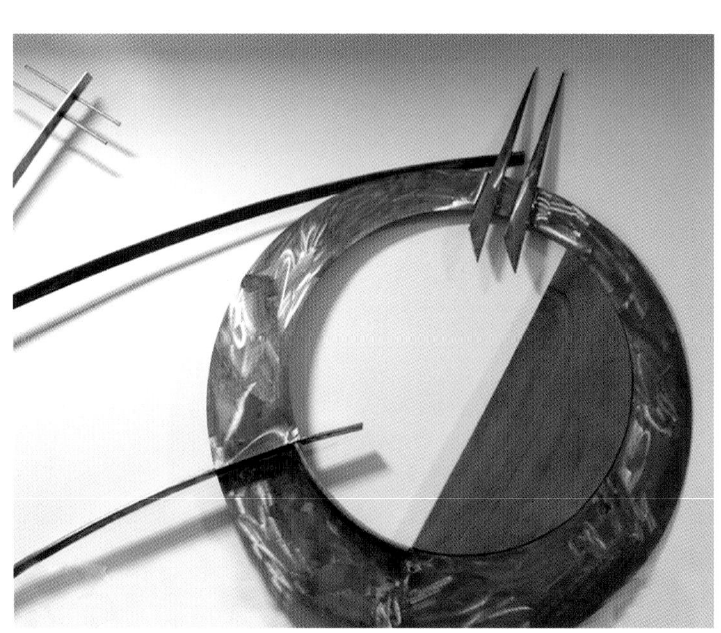

JAMES FINTAN LALOR

County Council Buildings, JFL Avenue, Portlaoise

Bronze figure of the journalist and revolutionary, who was born in Raheen in 1807.

Rory Breslin

THE CHALLENGE
Portlaoise College, Mountrath Road, Portlaoise
David Annand

TWO WORLDS
Court Square, Stradbally
Henk Korthuys

GROWTH
Library and Arthouse, Court Square, Stradbally
Laser-cut stainless steel mounted on the courtyard wall, the artwork is a large piece that acts like a Rorschach inkblot. The positive and negative shapes and changing light on the polished metal surfaces allow people to see what they will.
James Hayes

The limestone chair in the background was installed to commemorate the visit of President Michael D. Higgins in June 2012, when he officially opened the refurbished Library and the new Arts Centre.
Gerard Mulhall

NEWGRANGE

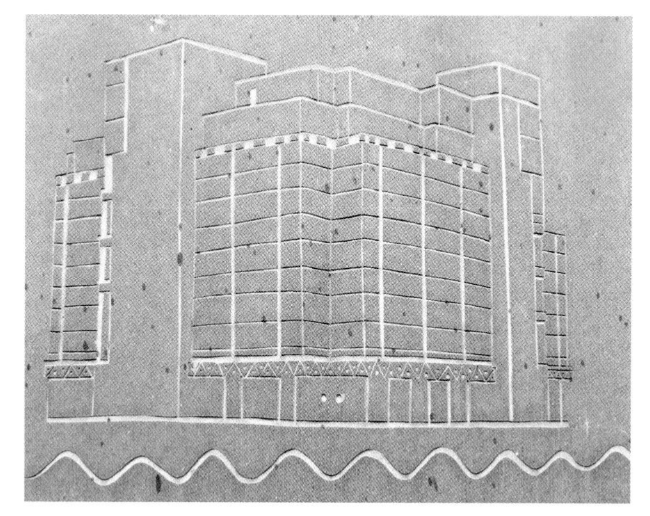

IFSC BUILDING, DUBLIN

THE STORY OF STONE

McKeon Stone, Brockley Park, Stradbally

Small selection from a series of limestone panels stretching along the street front of McKeon Stone. This is the longest piece of sculpture in the country, with the etchings showing the evolution of man's relationship with stone.

Dick Joynt

BUILDING CONSTRUCTION

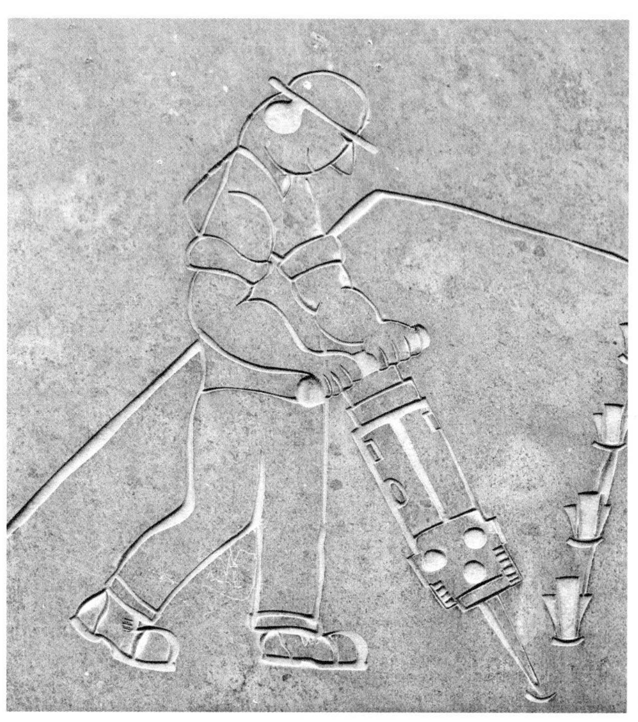

CONSTRUCTION

Longford

CORNCRAKES
Corncrake Meadows Estate, Abbeyshrule
Bog oak corncrake cluster to complement the seating and picnic area. The original field here was marshy, making it a suitable habitat for the corncrake.
Brendan Collum

GENERAL SEÁN MACEOIN
Ballinalee
Bronze on a limestone base. The anvil on which MacEoin's hand is resting is cast from a mould of the one he used as a youth. He is holding a copy of the Treaty, and his head is facing Clonfin. The names of the members of the North Longford Flying Column who took part in the Clonfin ambush are carved on the plinth.
Rory Breslin

SALMON
Abbeyshrule
Bog oak.
Brendan Collum

THE TRAVELLER
Main Street, Ballymahon
Oliver Goldsmith in bronze on limestone, his satchel on the ground beside him with a flute resting on top. Based on the theme of his poem 'The Traveller'.
Éamonn O'Doherty

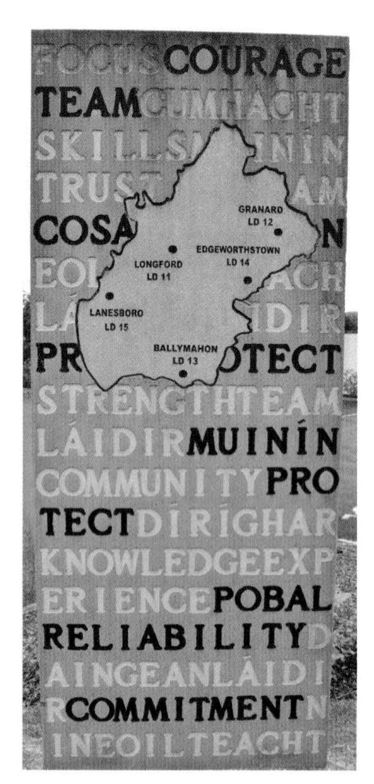

COMMEMORATIVE STONE
Fire Station, Edgeworthstown
The north-facing façade of the slab is covered in words associated with the Fire Service, with a map of Longford in the centre.
Mel French

MARIA EDGEWORTH
N4, Edgeworthstown
The eighteenth-century writer leaning against a bronze and concrete arch.
Mel French

SÍOL / SEED
Commemorative Garden, Great Water Street, Longford
Bronze on limestone plinth, the leaning figures spreading seeds suggest the work of the Tidy Towns Committee, digging, planting, lifting and painting. Gifted by Irish Business Against Litter to the Tidy Towns Committee of Ireland's tidiest town in 2015.
Patrick O'Loughlin

THE SENTINEL
River Walk, Lanesborough
Kevin Casey

THE WOOING OF ÉTAIN
Great Water Street, Longford
The myth of Midir and Étain—a story of love, betrayal, magic spells and all sorts of goings-on.
Pat Taaffe

HIDDEN LANDSCAPE
N5 Longford Bypass
Upper portion of a giant corten steel violin, sited as though it has been partly unearthed by the cut-away embankment. It alludes to the lost rural tradition of the *céilí* and crossroad gatherings before the present era of motorways.
Alex Pentek

EMIGRATION SUITE—LONGFORD'S GIFT TO THE WORLD
Canal Court Walk, Longford
Four bronze suitcases on limestone bases, a celebration of the contribution of Longford emigrants to the world. Each suitcase has a negative space in which is portrayed a small bronze vignette depicting some of their positive achievements.
Mel French

THE EMIGRANTS
Centenary Square, Longford
Bronze on limestone, a standing male looking east and a seated female looking west, each holding a ticket for a Cunard liner.
Rory Breslin

IF
Strokestown Road, Longford
Physical manifestation in stainless steel of the negative space between the letters 'I' and 'F'.
Joe and Pat Walker

PAT FITZGERALD
Rue Noyal Chatillon, Longford
The long-distance athlete was born at Lisduff Hill in 1847.
Artist's name unknown to the author

Louth

BRADÁIN/SALMON
Promenade, Blackrock
Kilkenny blue limestone piece representing the eighteenth-century fishing origins of the village.
Richard Perry

MILLENNIUM SUNDIAL
Promenade, Blackrock
Large sundial celebrating the millennium, the gnomon being a bronze female figure named Aisling. Instructions on how the sundial works are provided nearby.
Tanya Nyegaard

THE COCKLE-PICKERS

Promenade, Blackrock

Interwoven stainless steel piece. Cockle-picking in this area can be traced back to medieval times, evident from the middens and mounds of cockle shells still to be seen here. During the Famine cockles were the only source of food for many local families.

Micheál McKeown

GREETINGS
Clos na Manach, Carlingford
Steel abstract in blue, green and white.
Caroline McCarthy

CARLINN
Village Green, Carlingford
Stainless steel village sign.
Jim Collins

TÁIN **POEM**
John Kirk Park, Clogherhead
Bronze relief, with lines from the *Táin*, set into a wall in the housing scheme.
Jane Murtagh

GUIDING STAR
Port Oriel Harbour, Clogherhead
Cast-iron starfish.
Rachel Joynt

COLLANN
The Square, Collann
Stainless steel village sign.
Jim Collins

THE SOURCE
St Oliver's Community College, Drogheda
Bronze.
Ronan Halpin

***AN TÁIN BÓ CÚAILGNE*, THE BROWN BULL OF COOLEY**
The Bush, Cooley Peninsula
Represents the saga of Queen Maedbh and her husband Ailill and their row about riches. He owned a bull and she did not, so she sent her warriors to find a mighty one; when they did, she took the animal by force from its owner in what became known as the Cattle Raid of Cooley. The bulls had a great fight that ended in Maedbh's brown bull killing Ailill's white one.
Artist's name unknown to the author

CERCURILE VIETI
Educate Together National School, Aston Village, Drogheda
Cast-bronze, powder-coated mild steel. The form of the sculpture is informed by the ethos of the school: child-centred, co-educational, multi-denominational and democratically run.
Mark Ryan and Maree Hensey

LANTERN
Millmount Tower, Millmount, Drogheda
Bronze lantern piece on top of the tower.
Ronan Halpin

TONY 'SOCKS' BYRNE
North bank of the Boyne, Drogheda
The boxer who won bronze at the 1956 Olympic Games in Melbourne.
Laury Dizengremel, Zhang Yaxi and Shen Xiaonan

JOEY MAHER

North bank of the Boyne, Drogheda

World handball champion in Toronto in 1967. Erected to mark the 40th anniversary of his world handball achievements (1967–2007).

Laury Dizengremel

CONVERSATION CIRCLE

Ice House Hill Park, Dundalk

Five redwood and oak vessel seats set in a circle. The title was inspired by a circular stone-walled area of the same name at Arrowmount School of Arts and Crafts, Tennessee, where students sit and chat.

Liam O'Neill

DREAM GATES

Aisling Park, Dundalk

Pair of decorative stainless steel gates on limestone pillars.

Denis O'Connor

GARDA
Ice House Hill Park, Dundalk
Memorial to Martin Naughton and all members of the Garda Síochána who served in Dundalk since the foundation of the state.
Tanya Nyegaard

RIVER GODS
Barton Park, Dundalk
Three of a series of red-brick figures set on the wall of the small park leading into the estate.
Catherine Synnott

GUARDIANS OF THE THRESHOLD
Park Street, Dundalk
Decorative gates featuring two stylised heads.
Ronan Halpin

AN TÁIN
Market Square, Dundalk
Selection from a set of nine figures in bronze and glass.
John Behan

LONGA FAOI SHEOL
Lios Dubh Estate, Dundalk
Stainless steel abstract.
Jon Barlow Hudson

SOFA
Mullaharlin Park, Dundalk
Bronze three-seater sofa, cast from an existing sofa belonging to a resident of the estate.
Caroline McCarthy

RIASTRAD
Market Square, Dundalk
Murals including the Morrigan (the Celtic raven goddess) and Queen Maedbh's Brown Bull of Cooley.
Barry Finnegan and Killian Walsh

ABSTRACTION OF NEWGRANGE
Scoil Uí Mhuirí, Dunleer
The central angled slope simulates the light projecting deep into the central passage tomb, and the two triangular pieces that traverse the main piece are indicators of the glyph shapes on the entrance stone at Newgrange.
Cathail Kierans

THE WARRIORS
Market Square, Dundalk
One of two bronze-mounted lighting structures marking the entrance to Clanbrassil Street.
Artist's name unknown to the author

DUNLEER DRAWINGS

Shamrock Grove, Dunleer

Selection of ceramic tiles from a collection on the walls of the estate.

Hugh Lorigan and Emer Toomey

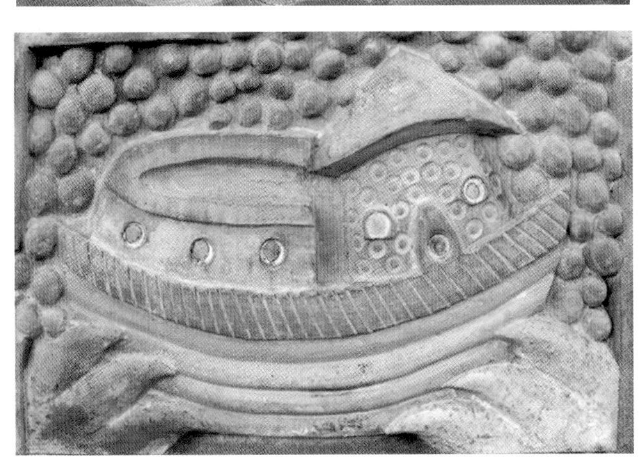

FELDA
St Fursey's National School, Marlbog Road, Haggardstown
Stainless steel.
Jim Collins

SALMON WEATHER-VANE
Cloughmore Cottages, Omeath
Bronze.
Jane Murtagh

VERE FOSTER
Tallantstown
Life-size bronze figure of the founder of the INTO. Born in Amsterdam of an Irish father, he left the UK Diplomatic Corps to help Famine victims on his brother's estate in this area. Concerned by reports of the conditions on the 'coffin ships', he travelled on one himself. He also founded the Irish Female Emigration Fund in 1852, and helped young women to emigrate to Canada on the first ship leaving that year.
Ann Meldon Hugh

RAVEN TREE
Rath View, Termonfeckin
Stainless steel tree and birds. The town name is linked to St Feichín, whose name means 'little raven'.
Denis O'Connor

Meath

HIMSELF

Ashbourne town centre

Larger-than-life-size bronze of Arkle, the greatest steeplechaser of all time, with Pat Taaffe, the jockey who rode him into the history books. During his state visit to Britain, President Higgins presented a miniature of this piece to Queen Elizabeth on behalf of the Irish people.

Emma MacDermott

THRESHOLD OF FREEDOM

Rath Cross, Ashbourne

Commemorating the Battle of Ashbourne, one of the most significant events outside Dublin in the 1916 Rising. The Irish Volunteers, commanded by Thomas Ashe, conducted a raid on the RIC barracks north of Ashbourne. Ashe's poem 'Let me carry your cross for Ireland, Lord' inspired the design, which shows him carrying a cross, and the piece is topped by an image of Róisín Dubh.

Peter Grant

MOL AN ÓIGE
Community School, Eightyeight Acres, Athboy
Two bronze student figures surrounded by books, satchel and sporting equipment.
Ann Meldon Hugh

WHEN THE WIND BLOWS
Scoil Oilibhéir Naofa, Coast Road, Bettystown
Bronze and wood seat installation taking the shape of a breaking wave and windswept trees.
Barry Linnane

RABBIT
M2 Junction 3, Ashbourne exit
Corten steel plate, this is a site-specific piece inspired by an origami rabbit created by David Shall.
Alex Pentek

MARE AND FOAL
Kribensis Manor, Williamstown Stud, Clonee
Two red metal pieces depicting a mare and foal located inside the entrance of a gated estate. The land was originally owned by a stud farmer.
Mark Ryan

COTHÚ / NURTURE
Gaelscoil Thulach na nÓg, Rooske Road, Dunboyne
A divided standing stone with a bronze tree in the centre. The stone symbolises the school and parents nurturing each child yet giving them room to grow; the tree represents each individual student.
Orla de Brí

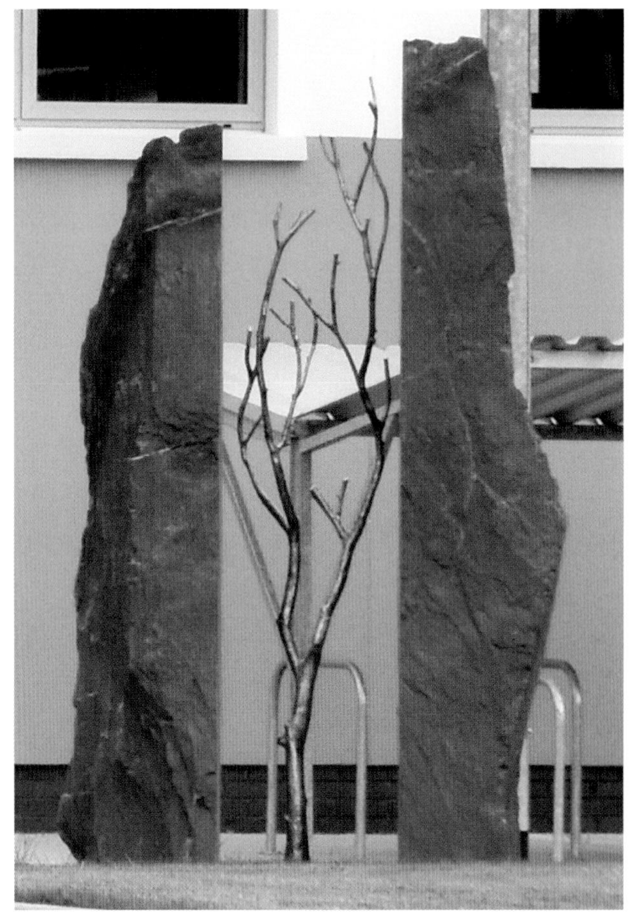

THE FAMILY
The Mound, Duleek
Stainless steel figures of father and mother with three children.
Maurice Harron

SEÁN BOYLAN
Dunboyne Castle
The football manager who was entered into the GAA Hall of Fame in recognition of his services to Meath football.
Artist's name unknown to the author

SPRING TO AUTUMN
Main Street, Dunshaughlin
Life-size bronze figures of an old man and a toddler, with footprints and poetry on the limestone base.
Ann Meldon Hugh

THE KELLS PANELS
Kells
Patrick Morris with students from Kells Youthreach, assisted by Mark Rathbone

TRIFOLIUM SCABRUM
Village Garden, Julianstown
The inspiration for this patinated bronze piece came from the scarce plant 'rough clover', which has been sighted at Julianstown bridge.
Rory Breslin

FLIGHT OF BIRDS
Moynalty
Bronze series of birds and bulrushes over a central pool. *Maigh nEalta*, meaning 'flock of birds', is the Irish for Moynalty.
Betty Newman Maguire

DEARFACHAS UAILLMHIAN BRÓD
Coláiste na hInse, Coast Road, Bettystown
Depicts three horses prancing in the waves, each one representing a word from the school motto: *dearfachas, uaillmhian* and *bród* (positivity, ambition and pride). Constructed of semi-fossilised bog woods (oak, yew and pine) revealed in Tipperary bogs during land clearance and turf-cutting.
Lynn Kirkham

MAISIÚIL / BECOMING
Kennedy Plaza, Navan
Fountain in which a bronze figure is set on a Kilkenny limestone base. The water flows over the stone and back, and is unique in that there is no pool of water. I just pretended that there was a fountain on the day I photographed the piece!
Betty Newman Maguire

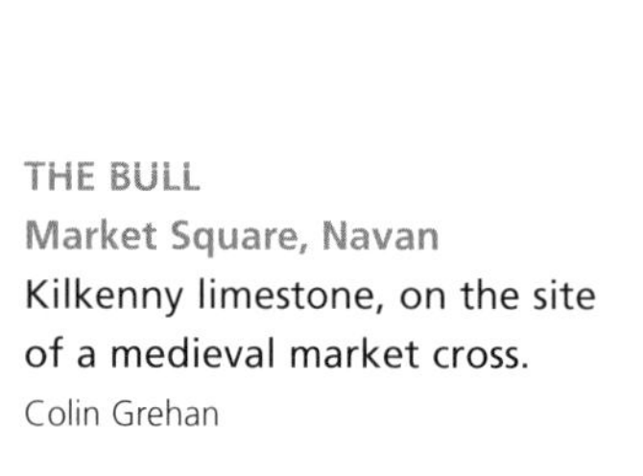

THE BULL
Market Square, Navan
Kilkenny limestone, on the site of a medieval market cross.
Colin Grehan

ON THE GREAT WIDE OPEN
Kells Road Roundabout, Navan
Kilkenny limestone piece recognising those who dedicated their lives to the mining industry in the area. The figure represents the movement of the stone from one location to another.
Patrick Barry

O'CAROLAN
Beside the Fire Station, Nobber
Bronze of the famous piper Turlough O'Carolan.
Ann Meldon Hugh

LAURENCE GILSON
Church Street, Oldcastle
Laurence Gilson bequeathed money towards the building of a school, completed in 1832, in his home town. The bronze sculpture shows him presenting the key of education to a girl and boy.
Ann Meldon Hugh

SPIRIT OF CREATIVITY
Loughcrew Gardens, Oldcastle
Bronze on steel ring.
Ann Meldon Hugh

CÚCHULAINN
Loughcrew Gardens, Oldcastle
The Irish mythological hero, gifted with superhuman strength, speed and hurling skill.
Ann Meldon Hugh

PERCH

Jamestown Roundabout, Ratoath

A blue curved steel arc with a seated bronze female figure on top, observing life from her elevated perch. The piece is about taking time to appreciate the beauty and uniqueness of your surroundings.

Orla de Brí

1798 BLACKSMITH

Curragha, Ratoath

Commemorating a young local blacksmith, Paud O'Donoghue, who took part in the 1798 rebellion.

Brendan Walshe

FREE SPIRIT

Slane Whiskey, Slane Castle

The horse, made from old whiskey barrels and steel plate, represents power, energy and forward thinking. She is also a reminder of the importance of the horse in the history of Slane Castle. The sculpture stands in a garden created by Daphne Shackleton, surrounded by old stable yards, carriage-houses and barns, originally designed by Capability Brown.

Lynn Kirkham

AT THE END OF THE DAY

Knightsbrook Roundabout, Trim

Kilkenny limestone, fabricated zinc and copper.

Patrick Barry

OUR LADY OF TRIM

Maudlin Cemetery, Trim

This cemetery is on the site of a leper hospital of the 1300s, Mary Magdalene Leper Hospital. In 1976 the local people commissioned the bronze commemorative piece.

Christopher Ryan

MAEL SEACHNAILL, HIGH KING OF IRELAND

Beside the playground in Trim

Mael Seachnaill was king of Meath (980–1002) and high-king of Ireland (1014–22).

James McKenna

Offaly

LIFE SIGNS
Community Nursing Unit, Birr
Copper life signs.
Paul Finch and Lynn Kirkham

JOHN FARRELL'S FIELD
Birr
Bronze statue of a hurler of that time, commissioned to mark the site of the first All-Ireland hurling final, played in 1888.
Mark Rode

LOOKING TO THE FUTURE
Dublin Road, Birr
Gateway sculpture, bronze life-size figures.
Ann Meldon Hugh

LOUGH BOORA DISCOVERY PARK

PASSAGE

The goal was to create a work that served as a visual and physical entrance into a particular landscape: a trench cut into an existing turf bank, floored with rail track, lined with sleepers. Beyond the passage three vertical rails reach skyward, and beyond these a trail into the forest.

Alan Counihan

SYSTEM NO. 30

Made from pieces of scrap collected on the site, the disc lends itself to the idea of a skimming stone bouncing over the surface of the canal. The sculpture tells part of the story of the mechanised harvesting of peat imposing itself on the bog: for over 50 years it travelled across the surface, using the land as a source of fuel.

Julian Wild

TIPPLER BRIDGE

This piece was influenced by the Nissan huts used in the 1940s/50s to house Bord na Móna workers during the peat harvest at Boora. Fabricated from a recycled tippler, which was used at the Ferbane power plant to unload peat from the incoming carriages. The piece combines the functional, i.e. bridge, shelter and bird hide, with a sculptural industrial aesthetic.

Kevin O'Dwyer

RAISED CIRCLE

Hundreds of miles of rails traverse our bogs, as narrow-gauge locomotives go to and fro pulling trains of turf wagons to power stations. The piece, fabricated from this narrow-gauge rail, floats one metre above the landscape and is painted the 'Bord na Móna yellow' that is found on everything from locomotives to turf-harvesting machinery.

Maurice MacDonagh

LOUGH BOORA DISCOVERY PARK

BOG OAK BRIDGE

The rustic bridge is made from a recycled steel bridge base that was once used for movement of light-gauge engines and trailers across the bogs in the 1940s. The bogwood uprights come from Drinagh Bog and carbon dating has shown them to be over 4,000 years old; the pine handrail was found in Killiun Bog at the firing range used by British soldiers from Crinkle Barracks in the late 1800s.

Don O'Boyle

THE PILGRIM

Clonmacnoise, Offaly

Bog oak figure of a pilgrim. Aedh, son of the chief of Oriel, died on pilgrimage in AD 606.

Jackie McKenna

PLAQUE

Arts and Heritage Centre, Ferbane

Mary Ward was born in Ferbane in 1827. She was a scientist, artist, author and naturalist, who published several books and had eight children. She was a cousin of Lord Rosse and frequently visited Birr Castle. On one such visit she died in 1869, in the world's first car accident. The *King's County Chronicle* gave a detailed report of the accident, including the comment that 'she has been so prematurely hurried into eternity'.

FUINNEAMH AN SAOIL
Gallen Community School, Ferbane
Fabricated and powder-coated steel, cast and patinated bronze. The sculpture represents the school: its vibrancy, energy and commitment to the values of creativity, diversity and inclusiveness, as well as its location close to the River Brosna.
Mark Ryan and Maree Hensey

MICK THE MILLER
Village Green, Killeagh
Bronze memorial to one of the most famous greyhounds ever, who won 51 of 68 races in Ireland and the UK. He was a direct descendant of the equally legendary Master McGrath, who is commemorated with statues in Lurgan and Dungarvan. They are the only racing greyhounds remembered in this way in Ireland.
Elizabeth O'Kane

BARACK AND MICHELLE OBAMA
Obama Plaza, Moneygall
The 44th president of the United States and his wife visited the town in May 2011. The president's great-great-great-grandfather, Falmouth Kearney, son of the town's shoemaker, emigrated to the US in the aftermath of the Famine.
Mark Rode

FREE SPIRIT
Garda Station, Tullamore
Bronze.
Cathy Carman

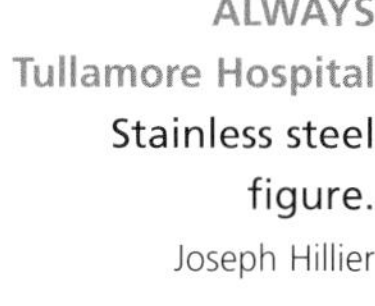

NOW, THEN, AND ALWAYS
Tullamore Hospital
Stainless steel figure.
Joseph Hillier

SLOW RELEASE OF DOVES
Hospital healing garden, Arden Road, Tullamore
Twelve sets of hands holding doves, carved from Italian Carrara marble.
Designed by Niamh Callery and sculpted by Ciaran O'Brien for the Friends of Tullamore Hospital

Westmeath

COUNT JOHN McCORMACK

Civic Buildings, Athlone Square

Bronze and limestone figure of the famous Irish tenor, who died in 1945.

Rory Breslin

MARIST BROTHER

St Mary's Square, Athlone

Erected to mark the role of the Marists in fostering education, culture and sport in the Athlone area over a 125-year period.

Mark Rode

ICARUS

Ballinahown Sculpture Park

This park was the location of the town's last forge, which closed in the 1950s. The sculpture was commissioned to commemorate the forge, and sits on an old stone piece discovered near the local church.

Dan Edwards

WOOD CARVINGS
Ballinahown Park
Richie Clarke

DÚN NA SÍ HERITAGE PARK, MOATE

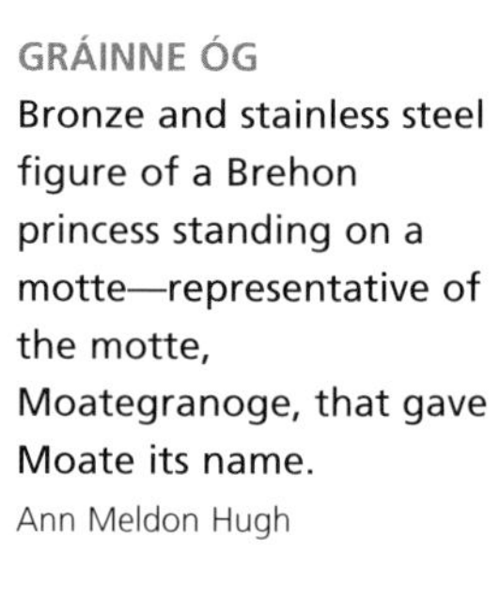

GRÁINNE ÓG
Bronze and stainless steel figure of a Brehon princess standing on a motte—representative of the motte, Moategranoge, that gave Moate its name.
Ann Meldon Hugh

TOTEM POLE
Kilcormac Secondary School Students

DÚN NA SÍ HERITAGE PARK, MOATE

LOCKS COB
Moate Community School Students

HERON
Pamela Keogh with Moate Community School Students

LUGH
Lugh, the Celtic sun-god, emerging from the hill with his spear—a 4,000-year-old piece of bog oak.
Patsy Preston

PIKE ON A BIKE
Moate Community School Students

GAME PIECE
Civic Offices, Mount Street, Mullingar

A bronze replica of a Viking-era bronze and bone board-game piece found in an archaeological dig in the area and now housed in the National Museum. The original piece is 25mm high.

Dony MacManus

SILVER BROSNA
Town Park, Mullingar

Stainless steel and bronze double-sided piece celebrating the history and beauty of the River Brosna and its importance to the town as a place of trade and industry.

Ann Meldon Hugh

MILLWHEEL FAMINE MEMORIAL
The Square, Mullingar
This stone and bronze sculpture commemorates the effects of the Famine on the area, and the millwheel ties the piece to Mullingar through the legend of St Colman. The hands are the hands of Leamhan—Elm—who inscribed her mark on such a stone.
Gerard Leslie

STREAM SPIRE
Town Park entrance, Mullingar
Cathal McCarthy

JOE DOLAN
Market Square, Mullingar
Bronze sculpture of the well-known singer (1939–2007).
Carl Payne

BAIL Ó DHIA ORAIBH GO LÉIR A CHÁIRDE
Cusack Park, Mullingar
Micheál O'Hehir, well-known GAA and racing commentator and journalist. In 1963 he faced his toughest broadcast, when John F. Kennedy was assassinated while Micheál was on holiday in New York. He was asked by RTÉ to provide commentary on the funeral, and he later described the five-hour live broadcast as the most moving and demanding of his career.
Mel French

WAY AHEAD
N4, Mullingar
Corten steel piece representing the legendary figures of Aoibh and the Children of Lir, depicting her children as departing swans. A symbolic arm signals to travellers their proximity to Mullingar and Lough Derravaragh, the home of the myth.
Bob Quinn

DOUBTING THOMAS
Church Grounds, Rosemount
This piece refers to St Thomas, the sceptical Apostle.
Richie Clarke

Wexford

FAUSCAILT
Larkin's Cross, Barntown
Known locally as 'the pikemen', this piece commemorates the 1798 Rebellion. Five larger-than-life bronze figures, each holding an extended pike.
Éamonn O'Doherty

HARMONY OF LEAVES
The Mall, Bunclody
Two bronze lime tree leaves and three large spheres on a granite base.
Declan Breen

WWII BOMBING MEMORIAL
Campile, Wexford

The sculptor carved the centre piece from an extremely rare marble called Breccia Medicea. He commissioned Anika Lintermann to describe in lettering on two slabs of Carrara marble a tragedy that occurred on 26 August 1940, when Campile was bombed by the German Luftwaffe and three local women were killed. The work was done in the Nicoli Studios in Carrara, a UNESCO World Heritage site. Commissioned by John Summers.

Ciaran O'Brien and Anika Lintermann

UNTITLED
Duncannon seafront

Three aluminium semicircles in primary colours.

Artist's name unknown to the author

HEDGEHOG
N11 Gorey Bypass

Corten steel plate, inspired by the origami of John Richardson. This is a landmark piece that light-heartedly reflects the surrounding rural area and community as a place of natural beauty which we must take care of.

Alex Pentek

TOUR DE FRANCE
The Fair Green,
Enniscorthy
Bronze image of a cyclist.
Mark Rode

CHERRIES
Presentation Park,
Enniscorthy
Three large black cherries
in Kilkenny limestone.
Martin Lyttle

QUIET MIND
EPA Building,
Johnstown Castle,
Wexford
Bronze.
Orla de Brí

AM AGUS SPÁS
Andy Doyle Close,
Enniscorthy
Kilkenny limestone fish symbolising the river flowing and life going on. The piece includes details of the death-mask of Cromwell, a pike symbolising Vinegar Hill, a dolmen and ogham script.
Philip Cullen

KELLY MEMORIAL
Killanne
John Kelly was wounded in the 1798 Rebellion. After the fall of Wexford he was dragged from his hospital bed, tried and hanged on Wexford Bridge. His exploits are commemorated in Patrick Joseph McCall's famous ballad 'Kelly the Boy from Killanne'.
Artist's name unknown to the author

JFK MEMORIAL
The Quay, New Ross
Life-size bronze of John F. Kennedy, 35th president of the United States, in front of a curved limestone wall featuring relief images and text. The bronze podium is on the spot where JFK spoke in June 1963 and beside where his great-grandfather emigrated to the US in 1848. Less than six months after his visit to his ancestral home Kennedy was assassinated in Dallas.
Ann Meldon Hugh

RAPHAEL'S HEALING GARDEN
Oylegate
The three sculptures show the Old Testament characters of Tobias, the Archangel Raphael and Tobias's little dog, which follows them both. When Tobias, who is on a long journey to seek healing for his blind father, is attacked by an enormous fish that tries to devour him, Raphael appears and saves him. This expresses the good and the bad experiences we have as we go through life. Commissioned by Revd James Cogley.
Ciaran O'Brien

TREE OF LIFE GARDEN
Oylegate
Italian Carrara marble and Glenbrien granite. Commissioned by Revd James Cogley.
Ciaran O'Brien

IRISH COUNTRYWOMEN'S ASSOCIATION
Oylegate
Unveiled in 2010 to commemorate 100 years of Oylegate Irish Countrywomen's Association, the longest-running guild in the country.
Carved in China

BY HOOK OR BY CROOK
Mill Road, Wexford
Corten stainless steel, with oak detail, the piece is influenced by the agricultural machinery and equipment produced by Pierce Engineering, a firm that was located on this site and closed in the 1980s.
John Atkin

SOLSTICE

County Buildings, Newtown Road, Carricklawn, Wexford

Bronze female figure poised in an almost enclosed circle.

Rowan Gillespie

NICKY RACKARD

Selskar Square, Wexford

A tribute to one of the county's great hurlers.

Mark Richards

LILY OF THE VALLEY

Mercy Primary School, St John's Road, Wexford

Wild Metal

LOCKOUT GATE

The Faythe, Wexford

A chained gate with an archway depicting workers commemorates the 100th anniversary of the lockout in Wexford. Two local iron foundries locked out 700 employees for over six months because they sought the right to join a trade union.

Peter Hodnett

Wicklow

ROTATIONS IN SPACE I
Arklow Shipping, North Quay, Arklow
The form is generated by the locus of a series of points moving in space.
Colm Brennan

AN SAIGHDIÚIR
Glendalough Road, Ashford
Cedar carving based on images of sixteenth-century Irish soldiers in Gaelic dress.
Séighean Ó Draoi

BUTTERFLIES
Arklow Bypass
Michael Johnson

STANDING STONES
Ashford Park

Five standing stones with wildlife themes as a nature trail for children: ants, teasel, salmon, frogs and fox. The designs were a collaboration with two local artists, Paula Kearney and Anna Doherty Ward.

Séighean Ó Draoi

BRADÁN FEASA / SALMON OF KNOWLEDGE AND DOBHARCHÚ / OTTER

Ashford Bridge

Two limestone pieces commissioned by Ashford Tidy Towns to reflect the wildlife associated with the Vartry River, which flows through the town

Séighean Ó Draoi

ST KEVIN AND THE BLACKBIRD

Kilmagig Graveyard, Avoca

St Kevin and his blackbird in blue granite, and in need of an umbrella on a very damp day in Wicklow. The modern piece fits well with the old graveyard in this remote open spot above the woods.

Séighean Ó Draoi

OGHAM STONE

St Gerard's School, Thornhill Road, Bray

A cursing/wishing stone: the stone in the basin on top is turned sunwise three times to make a wish or prayer, and anti-sunwise to make a curse. They were common on old monastic sites and are thought to be pagan in origin. Commissioned by the class of 2016 as a parting gift and in commemoration of the 1916 Rising.

Séighean Ó Draoi

SUN BOUNCE AND SOLAR SEATS

St Kevin's Community College, Dunlavin

Six circular mirrors on an upturned stainless steel dial. The mirrors reflect the sun onto a target located in the shade and denote the monthly gradation of the sun and earth's relational movements. At noon on the first day of each month the sun's light is interrupted on its path to earth, where it illuminates a target fixed to the wall of the school. Around the arrangement are 'solar seats'—benches in wood, black granite, glass, mirror and copper, which heat up and cool down at different rates.

Paul Gregg

SILENT KEEPER

Schoolhouse for Art, Main Square, Enniskerry

Carved from oak, the symbol of strength and endurance, it is a representation of being in that silent space.

Conleth Gent

ST KEVIN

Glendalough

Kevin was born in AD498 and lived as a hermit in a cave, now known as St Kevin's Bed, in Glendalough valley, where he eventually set up a permanent monastery. He had a special bond with wildlife, and is often portrayed with a blackbird. Legend has it that the bird laid an egg in his hand, which was outstretched in prayer, and that he held that position until the hatchling emerged. Seamus Heaney wrote a poem about this event, exploring the relationship between meaning and myth.

Imogen Stuart

BEAR WITH BUCKET AND SPADE

Seafront, Greystones

Teddy is off to play on the beach!

Patrick O'Reilly

SHEKINA SCULPTURE GARDEN, GLENMALURE

This sculpture garden is the result of many years' work by Catherine McCann in acquiring some iconic pieces by great artists. In 1998 she generously donated the garden to the state, and the gift was received by the then Minister for Arts, Culture and the Gaeltacht, Michael D. Higgins. It is now the property of the Department of Culture, Heritage and the Gaeltacht, and is maintained by the Department's National Parks and Wildlife Service. In 2017 Michael D. Higgins, as president of Ireland, returned to Glenmalure to officially open the 'Shekina Exhibition', celebrating twenty years of the Sculpture Garden. Catherine McCann continues to be the curator of this exceptional home for art.

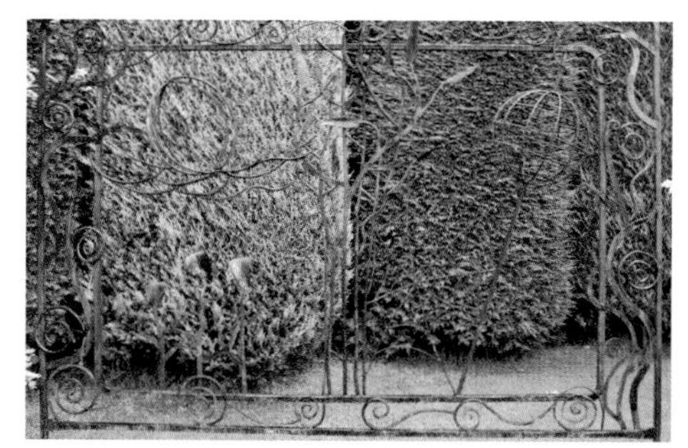

CREATION OF THE UNIVERSE
One of four wrought-iron screens based on the Bible's account of the creation of the universe.
Paul Page

UNTITLED
Bog yew piece, revealed by carbon dating to be 4,500 years old.
Michael Casey

UNTITLED
The sculptor was fascinated by the notion of the spiral.
Fred Conlon

CASADH NA GEALAI / TURNING OF THE MOON
Near the entrance to the sculpture garden, a Dublin granite piece based on the landscapes and seascapes of the sculptor's native Sligo.
Fred Conlon

OUR FRACTURED WORLD
Stainless steel globe.
Michael Foley

DESCENDING DOVE
The artist says that the Holy Spirit, symbolised here by a dove, is not seen; only His effect is felt.
Ken Thompson

WAVE
The ascending movement of each wave, represented by the seven prongs, soars towards their ending, spreading upward and outward.
Leo Higgins

SHEKINA SCULPTURE GARDEN, GLENMALURE

LOVERS
Not a pair of praying hands—the bronze piece is of the hands of a man and a woman clasping each other.
Imogen Stuart

DANCERS
Four dancers, each in a different pose.
Alexander Sokolov

UNTITLED
Irregular octagon of Dublin granite showing that the mass is completely altered by light coming through when a circle is cut in it. This was the first piece in the Shekina collection.
Cliodna Cussen

IN A SACRED GROVE
Carved from one of the last fragments of Dún Laoghaire granite, the front of the seat reveals two figures emerging from overarching trees.
James Gannon

SILVER FLAME
The slightest wind causes the flame to move, and when sunlight hits it a radiant effect is produced; as a consequence it is seen as an 'eternal flame'.
Alexandra Wejchert

COLOURS OF THE RAINBOW
The changing of the seasons influences the appearance of the mirrored parts of the piece.
Elke Westen

DREAMERS REST
The bench depicts the sculptor's wife and son just as they fell asleep.
Noel Scullion

SHEKINA SYMBOL
Enamelled work showing the fire symbol. Shekina, a feminine Hebrew word, is one of several used by Jews in naming God.
Anne Murphy

CHARLES STEWART PARNELL

Parnell Memorial Park, Rathdrum

Parnell, who was born in Avondale, was an Irish nationalist politician, a member of the British parliament, and leader of the struggle for Irish Home Rule in the late nineteenth century. His most famous quote, delivered in 1885, is: 'No man has a right to fix the boundary of the march of a nation; no man has a right to say to his country—thus far shalt thou go and no further'.

Fred Conlon

FAIR DAY

Rathdrum Square

Commemorating the markets held in the square. Inspired by students from the four local schools, who submitted designs under the theme 'fair day in Rathdrum': a sheep-farmer relaxes with his dog after selling his wool at the market.

Eleonora McNamara

PADDY GANESH

Victor's Way, Sallygap Road, Roundwood

Sculpted in Tamil Nadu, India, this is one of a group of nine Ganesh images and other works in a contemplative garden.

D.V. Murugan and T. Baskaran

UNTITLED

Coláiste Chill Mhantáin, Burkeen, Wicklow

An abstract interpretation of the school crest, the form resembles the bow of a boat, a wave. As the school community passes through the sculpture together they share a journey, conjuring a sense of togetherness, purpose and friendship.

Mark Ryan and Maree Hensey

AN LON DUBH, THE BLACKBIRD OF AVONDALE

Roundabout, Rathdrum

Jesmonite with a steel armature. Parnell was known as 'the Blackbird of Avondale', a bird that is a symbol of intelligence and wit.

Eleonora McNamara

Munster

Clare

THATCHED COTTAGE MURAL
Ballynacally
Elaine Gavin

SISTER OF MERCY
Clare Museum Building, Ennis
Set in the gable wall of the building, this small marble piece is one of the most delicate installations I have seen. Commissioned by the Ennis Sculpture Initiative.
Barry Wrafter

PAT O'DONNELL
White Strand, Killard, Doonbeg
Pat O'Donnell emigrated to the US in 1896 and progressed to captain in the New York police. He was an Olympic gold medallist and world record-holder in hammer-throwing.
Jim Connolly

DROMOLAND CASTLE WALLED GARDEN

Galvanised fencing-wire fairies on toadstools of jesmonite and fibreglass with a foam internal structure. The artist felt that the garden has a fairytale quality, so the fairy image seemed to be ideal for the space.

Carmel Doherty

A SPINE PATH
Entrance path to Library HQ, Mill Road, Ennis
Green slate path with bronze detail, resembling a book spine.
Rachel Joynt

CENTURIAL SPHERE
Club Bridge, Ennis
Commemorative piece for the centenary of the 1916 Rising. Internally illuminated galvanised and lacquered steel sphere. It carries lines from poems and songs celebrating the culture and tradition of various parts of Clare.
Conor and Paddy Murray

ÉAMON DE VALERA
Courthouse, Ennis
Bronze figure of the former president of Ireland.
Jim Connolly

DREAMBOAT
River walk, Mill Road, Ennis
Kilkenny limestone boat and cross with markings, including dress, star, map, heart etc., carved into the surface. These offer clues to the story the piece tells.
Fiona O'Dwyer

SLEEPY HEAD—HELPING HANDS
Parnell Street car park, Ennis
According to the artist, these pieces evolved almost accidentally as a result of his work with his assistant David McNamara.
Shane Gilmore

NATURE'S RHYTHM
Tulla Road, Ennis
Slim wood carving with indentation in front and spiral on top.
Mary Gilmore

CRAOLAGH
Park Avenue, Cappahard, Ennis
Colm Brennan

MICHAEL CUSACK
Cusack Park, Ennis
Michael Cusack was co-founder with Michael Davin of the Gaelic Athletic Association, and its first secretary.
Michael McTigue

FAMILY GROUP
Old Drumcliff Cemetery, Gort Road, Ennis
Shane Gilmore

MUTATION
Kincora Park, Ennis
Tall abstract piece.
Shane Gilmore

DAEDALUS, A MOMENT OF FLIGHT
Rocky Road Roundabout, Ennis
The sculptor titled this piece 'Daedalus' but the locals started calling it 'Icarus' and the name has stuck. For what it's worth, it looks like the face of an adult to me, but who am I to argue with the locals?
John Behan

BRIAN MERRIMAN
Ennistymon
Merriman was a teacher and Irish-language poet most famous for the great satirical poem *Chúirt an Mheán Oíche*, 'The Midnight Court'.
Shane Gilmore

CRANN A' GHRÁ / TREE OF LOVE
Kilbaha
Diarmuid and Gráinne in bronze and bog wood. The piece—and, indeed, the entire village—was badly damaged in the flooding caused by Storm Eleanor in 2014. Gráinne was still recovering when I was in the area, but she will return.
Jim Connolly

DOG ON A BENCH
Árd na Coille, Ennistymon
Declan Breen

CAT AND HARE
Near Kilbaha Gallery, Kilbaha
Bronze cat and hare. The bird is not a sculpture—he is just resting!
Seamus Connolly

STEEL STONE
St John Bosco Community College, Kildysart
Marie Brett

RICHARD HARRIS
Diamond Rocks, Kilkee
Richard Harris playing a local game, played against a wall with a tennis racquet.
Seamus Connolly

SAND CASTING
Smith's Garden, Kilkee
Bronze piece of a girl building a sandcastle on a limestone base.
Colin Johnston

AN CAILÍN BÁN

Ferry Terminal entrance, Killimer

In 1819 John Scanlan arranged for the murder of his sixteen-year-old wife, Ellen Hanley, who had eloped with him; his servant shot her and dumped her in the Shannon, but six weeks later her body washed ashore at Moneypoint. Both Scanlan, who was defended by Daniel O'Connell, and his servant, Sullivan, were convicted of the murder and hanged. Ellen, An Cailín Bán, is buried in nearby Burrane cemetery.

Jim Connolly

WOODEN PIECE WITH OGHAM

Ferry Terminal, Killimer

The names of counties Clare and Kerry are inscribed on the piece in ogham to represent the strong, centuries-old trading relationship between them.

Raymond Glynn

THE FIRST BREATH
Marina, Kilrush
Two bronze dolphins pushing the baby upwards to take its first breath.
Danny Osborne

1916 COMMEMORATIVE SCULPTURE
Beside the Boatyard, Kilrush
Paddy Murray

TWO DOLPHINS

Market Square, Kilrush

Bronze dolphins on a stainless steel plinth.

Mike Smith

RAMPANT GOAT

Lahinch Golf Course

Life-size bronze goat unveiled in 2017 as part of the club's 125th anniversary celebrations. Goats were a constant presence on the course in the 1950s.

Seamus Connolly

JOHN PHILIP HOLLAND
Liscannor
The local engineer who invented the submarine.
Shane Gilmore

SEISIÚN / SESSION
The Square, Lisdoonvarna
Bronze couple dancing, with musicians in the background.
Cliodna Cussen

FLIGHT
Skycourt Shopping Centre, Shannon Development
Joe Neeson

WILLIE CLANCY
Milltown Malbay
Bronze piece commemorating the great musician who was a native of the town. He began playing the tin whistle at the age of five, moved on to the flute and later became a renowned uilleann piper before his death in 1973 at the age of 55.
Shane Gilmore

Cork

CREAMERY
Ballyclough
Commissioned by Dairygold, this cast-bronze piece is on the site of the former Ballyclough Creamery near Mallow.
Kevin Holland

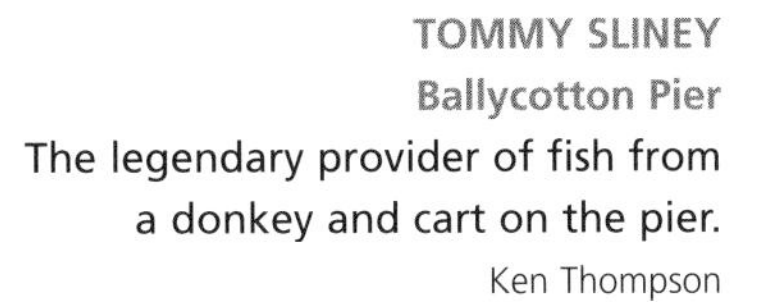

TOMMY SLINEY
Ballycotton Pier
The legendary provider of fish from a donkey and cart on the pier.
Ken Thompson

DANNO
Town centre, Ballydehob
Bronze life-size figure of local hero Danno O'Mahony, born in 1912. A professional wrestler who won the National Wrestling Association's World Heavyweight Title in Boston in 1935, he was also a champion weightlifter. He died in a car accident in 1950.
James McCarthy

THE BEACON

Entrance to Baltimore Harbour

This distinctive landmark looked surreal on a very foggy day. Built in about 1830, it was one of a series of lighthouses and navigational beacons forming a warning system around the Irish coast. Known locally as 'Lot's Wife', after the biblical woman who was turned into a pillar of salt.

Crowley Brothers

DR PAT O'CALLAGHAN

Banteer

Olympic gold medallist for the hammer throw in Amsterdam 1928—the first time the Irish tricolour was raised for a podium presentation at the Olympic Games—and Los Angeles 1932.

Barry Linnane

CAPTAIN FRANCIS O'NEILL

Captain O'Neill Memorial site, Tralibane, Bantry

Born in 1848, Francis O'Neill became Chicago's Chief of Police; he also collected and published thousands of Irish tunes.

Jeanne Rynhart

ST BRENDAN
Wolfe Tone Square, Bantry
Commissioned to mark the opening of the Gulf Oil Terminal on Whiddy Island in 1969.
Imogen Stuart

BANTRY BOATS
Bantry House, Seafield, Bantry
In Portuguese and Kilkenny limestones, the theme is taken from the image of a boat sailing on the vertical, as found carved on the Kilnaruane Pillar Stone nearby. A gift from UCC to mark the donation of the Bantry House archives to the Boole Library.
Jason Ellis

MILL COVE GALLERY AND GARDENS, BEARA

ZENGDI

Ceramic with concrete base. This is the tallest ceramic sculpture in the country, the work of an artist who has been sculpting for over 50 years.

Jim Turner

SENTINEL

The title of this Kilkenny limestone art-deco-influenced piece comes from the fact that it contains the four cardinal compass points, north, south, east and west. It reminded the artist of a sentry standing guard and watching in all directions.

Richie Healy

VENETIAN

Bronze.

Ken Drew

TWO FIGURES

Marble.

James Horan

FINDERS KEEPERS

Bronze with bronze base.

Ana Duncan

DEBS

Cold-formed and polished stainless steel on a brushed stainless and mild steel base.

Martin O'Keefe

BUTTEVANT TO DONERAILE
Bronze plaque commemorating the world's first recorded steeplechase in 1752—Buttevant to Doneraile—raced by Cornelius O'Callaghan and Edmund Blake.
James MacCarthy

THE VILLAGE FORGE
Bweeng, Cork
The sculptor, who lives locally, made this piece of a blacksmith, horse and anvil to commemorate the O'Mullane family, who worked a forge here from 1870 to 1957. He donated the piece when the villagers decided to install a sculpture to enhance the area.
William Sandham

THE DRAKE SAIL
Carrigaline
A stainless steel maritime sculpture beside the Owenabue River, commemorating the arrival of Sir Francis Drake in Cork Harbour in 1589 to escape the Spanish fleet. The accompanying plaque has an etching of Drake's original ship, the *Golden Hind.*
Peadar Drinan

BLARNEY CASTLE

CLASSICAL GROWTH
Steel-reinforced fibre concrete.
Ken Drew

MEADOW HARE
Bronze unique.
Ester Barrett

PREHISTORIC BIRD
Bog oak.
Pieter Koning

JULIET
Bronze.
Éamonn Ceannt

IGUANA
Mixed metals.
Nigel Connell Bass

IRISH WOLFHOUND
Galvanised wire.
Gwen Wilkinson

ARK OF THOUGHT
St James's Cemetery, Bandon Road, Chetwynd
Barry Linnane

CLOCH NA GCOILLTE
Emmet Square, Clonakilty
Unveiled by President Higgins on 5 May 2013 to commemorate the creation of the Borough of Clonakilty by charter on 5 May 1613.
Michael Warren

VINCENT O'BRIEN
Churchtown, Cork
The horse-trainer, who was born in Churchtown, was voted the greatest influence in horse-racing history in a worldwide poll hosted by the *Racing Post* in 2003.
Artist's name unknown to the author

WOODLANDS

Woodlands Estate, Skibbereen Road, Clonakilty

Three giant cast-bronze leaves creating a work that has meaning and interaction with children living nearby.

Alex Pentek

CURLEW
Gaelscoil Mhichil Uí Choileáin, Fernhill Road, Clonakilty
Edain Ní Dhómhnaill

MICHAEL COLLINS
Emmet Square, Clonakilty
National memorial statue unveiled by Liam Neeson on 22 August 2002, the anniversary of Collins's assassination. Neeson played the title role in the 1996 film *Michael Collins*, which also starred Aidan Quinn, Stephen Rea, Alan Rickman, Brendan Gleeson, Ian Hart and Julia Roberts.
Kevin Holland

SS *LUSITANIA* PEACE MEMORIAL

Casement Square, Cobh

The Cunard liner *Lusitania* was torpedoed by a German U-boat off the Cork coast on 7 May 1915, less than a year after the outbreak of World War I. It sank with the loss of 1,188 lives. Many of the bodies and survivors were brought ashore here, and 170 of the victims were buried in the local cemetery. This magnificent peace memorial honours the victims, those who helped in the rescue efforts, and all who assisted the survivors and buried the dead.

Jerome Connor

CHRISTY RING

Cloyne

Commemorating the great Cork hurler who, during a remarkable career, won eight All-Ireland medals.

Yann Renard Goulet

SONIA O'SULLIVAN

Town centre, Cobh

Bronze sculpture of the athlete who is a native of the town.

James McLoughlin

UNIVERSITY COLLEGE CORK

CONSTRUCTION NO. 5

This piece plays with the forms of classical columns. The selection of sheet aluminium as the material and the cradling of the fallen broken column between the four upright ones may evoke ideas of redundant orthodoxies. Donated to the college by Dr J.B. Kearney.

Ian Stuart

WORLD WAVES

Western Gateway Building, Western Road

Macrocarpa wood and steel framework. This piece represents all life and the Linnaean classification system: kingdom, phylum, class, order etc.

Con Gent and Paul Flynn

FEMALE NUDE

The Quad

Bronze.

Don Cronin

FIGURE TALKING TO A QUADRUPED

The Quad

Kilkenny limestone.

Michael Quane

DESERT ANT

Originally located at the business of philanthropist Dr Tom Cavanagh in Fermoy, where it stimulated reflection on the worlds of nature and manufacturing. He donated the painted steel piece to the college in 1995.

John Burke

ANNIE MOORE
Waterfront, Cobh

Bronze image of fifteen-year-old Annie Moore with her younger brothers Anthony and Philip, prior to departing on the SS *Nevada*. Annie was the first person admitted to the US through the new processing centre at Ellis Island on 1 January 1892. There is a complementary statue at Ellis Island: in Cobh she is glancing back, while on Ellis Island she is striding purposefully forward to her new life. It would be a very difficult one: she had eleven children, six of whom predeceased her, and she herself died of heart failure at 50.

Jeanne Rynhart

UNFURL
Ashton Comprehensive School, Blackrock Road, Ballintemple, Cork

Folded and perforated bronze.

Alex Pentek

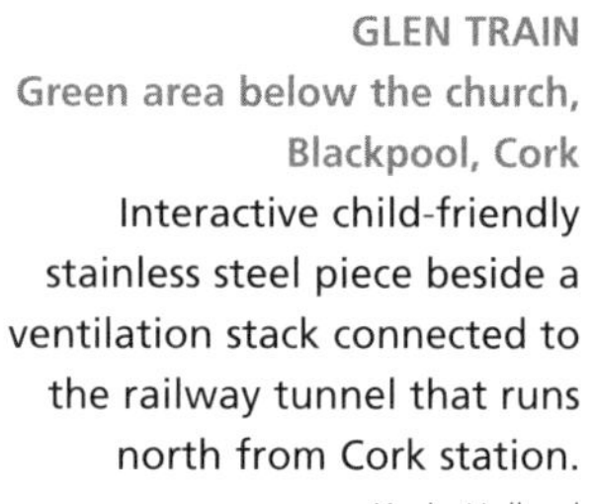

GLEN TRAIN
Green area below the church, Blackpool, Cork

Interactive child-friendly stainless steel piece beside a ventilation stack connected to the railway tunnel that runs north from Cork station.

Kevin Holland

LOST INDUSTRIES
Blackpool, Cork
Acknowledges the industrial heritage of the area, in particular whiskey, textiles and tanning. These industries were powered by water from the River Bride, so the piece incorporates river lines, a water-wheel, a pot still, a skyline of industrial buildings and a ladder, suggesting the regeneration of the area today.
Denis O'Connor

BULL AND DROVER
Watercourse Road, Blackpool
Sheet-bronze piece mounted on a gable wall of Maddens Buildings, built on what had been a green area famous for its cattle market.
Kevin Holland

BERYL
Revenue Commissioners, Assumption Road, Blackpool, Cork
Carved Kilkenny limestone on a Cork limestone base, this is a heroic-scale dog modelled on the artist's own wire-haired terrier, Beryl, and inspired by the fact that the building also houses customs dogs trained to detect contraband.
Alex Pentek

CHRISTY RING
The Airport, Kinsale Road, Cork
Commemorating the man who was probably Ireland's greatest-ever hurler and whose sporting career spanned about 30 years.
Seán McCarthy

EVENING ECHO

SEARCH FOR GOLD IN IRELAND

TITLE OF BRITISH QUEEN

NEW MOVE AGAINST CHURCH

THE *ECHO* BOY
St Patrick Street, Cork
Commemorating 150 years of the *Cork Examiner* and 100 years of the *Evening Echo*. The front page of the *Echo* is a replica of the newspaper of 20 February 1952.
Barry Moloney

REEDPOD
Lapps' Quay, Cork
Hand-forged copper over stainless steel.
Eilis O'Connell

LISTENING POSTS
Penrose Quay, Cork
Four stainless steel beacon-like pillars on the site of a traditional departure point for emigrant boats like the *Innisfallen* in the 1940s, '50s and '60s.
Daphne Wright

MARY ANNE—THE ONION SELLER
Bishop Lucey Park, Grand Parade, and Cornmarket Street, Cork
The city is fortunate to have two pieces commemorating the women dealers of the Coal Quay market—the original was cast in bronze by the artist in 1937. The piece at Bishop Lucey Park, dated 1985, was presented to the city by Sunbeam Wolsey, a factory that provided work for thousands of women from 1928 to 1995. The piece on Cornmarket Street, dated 1995, was presented to the city by a MacDonald's franchisee.
Seamus Murphy

REFLECTIONS

Fitzgerald Park, Cork

Irish limestone piece reflecting how we view ourselves differently from the way others see us, physically or mentally—our distorted reality, body-shaming issues, or when children feel excluded for various reasons.

James Horan

LILÍOCH

Parnell Bridge, South Mall, Cork

Commemorating the centenary of the 1916 Easter Rising, these two forms represent the two channels of the River Lee rising to form a budding lily, the symbol of the Rising.

Mick Wilkins

BRIAN QUILLIGAN

Salmon Weir, Western Road, Cork

Wood-carving of a resting fisherman, commemorating the artist's brother, who drowned while fishing here in 2011, and all who have lost their lives in the River Lee.

Mark Quilligan

CHA AND MIAH

Kingsley Hotel, Victoria Cross, Cork

This whimsical piece, named after two well-known Cork characters, was installed at the hotel to complement Oisín Kelly's famous piece, which was unveiled in front of the new County Hall across the road in 1968.

Brendan Byrne

MOTOR CYCLIST
Glenamoy Lawn, Old Youghal Road, Cork
Artist's name unknown to the author

CHILDREN PLAYING FOOTBALL
Scoil Naomh Eoin Easpal, Árd Bhaile, Cork
Ann Meldon Hugh

PATRICK KEOHANE
Barry's Point, Courtmacsherry
Keohane, who grew up here, was one of four Irishmen on Robert Scott's ill-fated 1910 Terra Nova Antarctic expedition. He was a member of the search party who found the frozen bodies of the Polar group and helped bury them. He afterwards served in both World Wars and died in 1950, aged 71. Michael Smith, the author of many outstanding books on the Polar explorers, told me that the image of the man looking out to sea comes from Keohane's own comment that he 'always wanted to see what was over the other side of the hill'—and he did!
Don Cronin

TWILIGHT HAUL

Dinish Island

Two bronze fishermen holding a boat aloft; one looks out to sea while the other looks back inland, symbolising the interdependence of land and sea in a fishing community. The sculpture was the initiative of the local branch of Mná na Mara, a support organisation for women involved in the fishing industry.

Barry Linnane

SAM MAGUIRE

Town Square, Dunmanway

Born in the town in 1879, Maguire was a well-known sportsman who played in All-Ireland finals from 1900 to 1903. On his death in 1927, a group of his friends presented a commemorative cup modelled on the Ardagh Chalice to the GAA for the annual All-Ireland Senior Football final.

Maurice Harron

LAST LIGHT SUNDIAL
Dursey Head
On 31 December 1999 ceremonies took place all over Ireland to commemorate the last sunset of the millennium. The final 'Last Light' event took place at Dursey Head in West Cork, where the latest sunset over Ireland occurred at 4.41pm. Commissioned by the National Millennium Committee.

THE TOWER
The Bridge, Fermoy
Mirrored, polished stainless steel piece made in response to the River Blackwater and the Fermoy Scheme for flood defence.
James Hayes

THE CUT
M8 between Fermoy and Mitchelstown
A large stainless steel stylised representation of the blades of a mower, it refers both to the breaking of the earth for tillage and the large earthworks that had to be undertaken to make this section of the motorway which literally cuts through the landscape.
Joe Neeson

BÓ BAINNE

Roundabout at Junction 14, M8, and Teagasc Dairy Research Centre, Moorepark, Fermoy

Five bog oak and galvanised steel dairy cows, three on the roundabout and two in the Teagasc Centre. Commissioned by Teagasc and Moorepark Farm Research Centre

Lynn Kirkham and Cathal O'Meara Landscape Architects

SURFBOARD

Inchydoney

Moss Gaynor, Mojo

THADY KELLEHER
Kanturk
Bronze piece commemorating the four-time winner of the Irish senior horse ploughing title and two-time winner of the international championship.
Don Cronin

HORSE AND RIDER
Innishannon
Bronze.
Don Cronin

THE WAVE
***Lusitania* Memorial Garden, Old Head of Kinsale**
Commemorating the sinking of the *Lusitania*.
Eithne Ring and Liam Lavery

MOSAIC MAP

Charlesfort, Kinsale

Inside the fort entrance, this ceramic map is more than art—it is a useful visitors' guide to the layout of the fort.

Joe Neeson

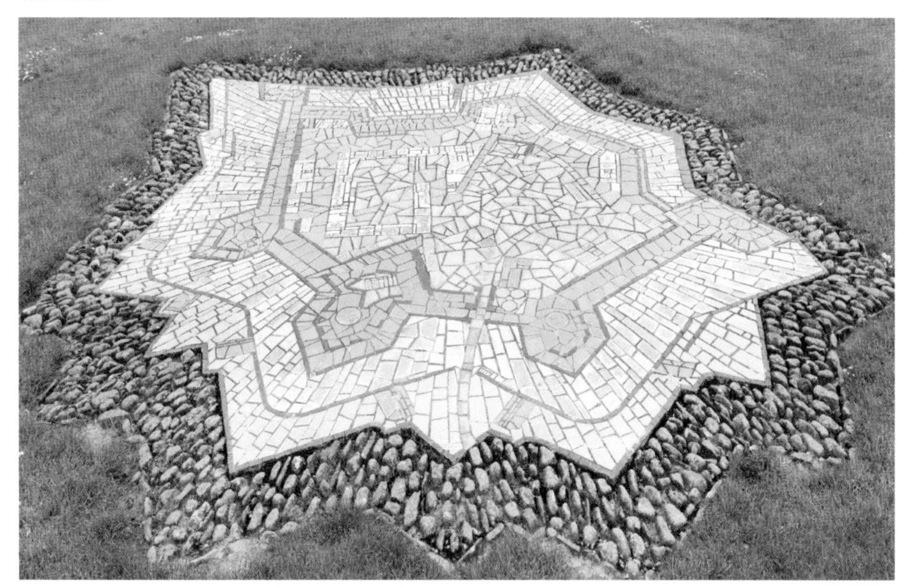

TUMBLING HELICOPTERS

St Colman's National School, Sleeveen East, Macroom

Stainless steel and bronze.

Don Cronin

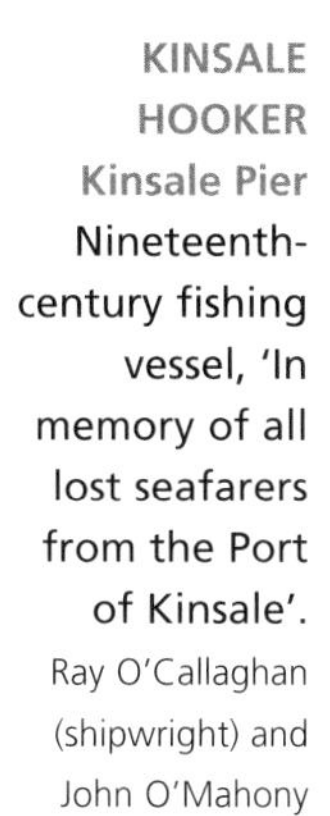

KINSALE HOOKER

Kinsale Pier

Nineteenth-century fishing vessel, 'In memory of all lost seafarers from the Port of Kinsale'.

Ray O'Callaghan (shipwright) and John O'Mahony

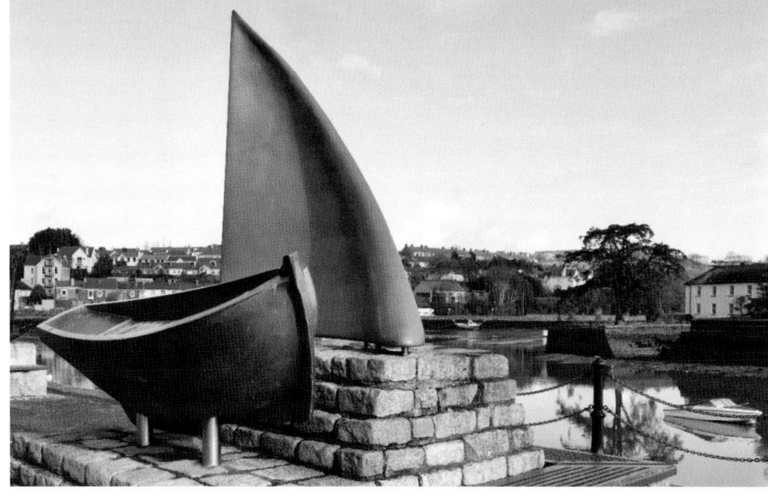

THE ANGEL OF THE CASSIAR MOUNTAINS

Riverside Way, Midleton

Nellie Cashman was born in Midleton in 1845 and her family fled the Famine in 1850. She acquired legendary status in US mining communities as a miner, nurse, businesswoman and philanthropist. She drove a dog team over 1,200km in seventeen days when she was 80! The US postal service issued a stamp in her honour, she was inducted into Alaska's Mining Hall of Fame and Tombstone annually celebrates 'Nellie Cashman Day'.

Michael Disley

GOOSE BOY

The Goose's Acre, Midleton

A boy and his geese on a clear October night. The piece reflects the traditional use of the area by locals grazing their geese.

Niall Bruton

KINDRED SPIRITS
Bailick Park, Midleton
Sunset at the stainless steel Choctaw feathers, a piece commemorating the generosity of the Choctaw nation who, soon after the devastation of their own Trail of Tears, collected $170 to assist victims of the Irish Famine.
Alex Pentek

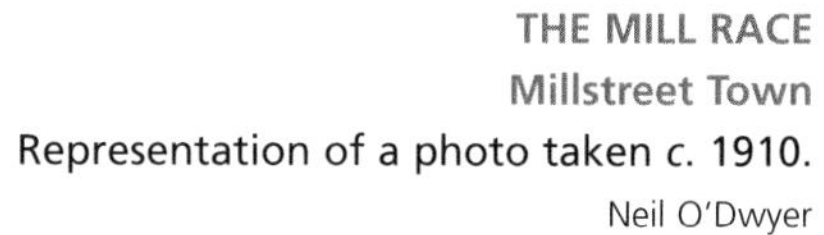

THE MILL RACE
Millstreet Town
Representation of a photo taken *c.* 1910.
Neil O'Dwyer

SHEEP
The Goose's Acre, Midleton
Four sheep encircling the base of a pillar.
Joe Neeson

ST FANAHAN

Main Street, Mitchelstown

St Fanahan with the symbols associated with him: a staff, based on a ninth-century crozier in the National Museum; a hound, in reference to the Irish of his name, Cú Bán, which means 'white hound'; and an eel, *eascann*, sometimes seen in St Fanahan's Well.

Cliodna Cussen

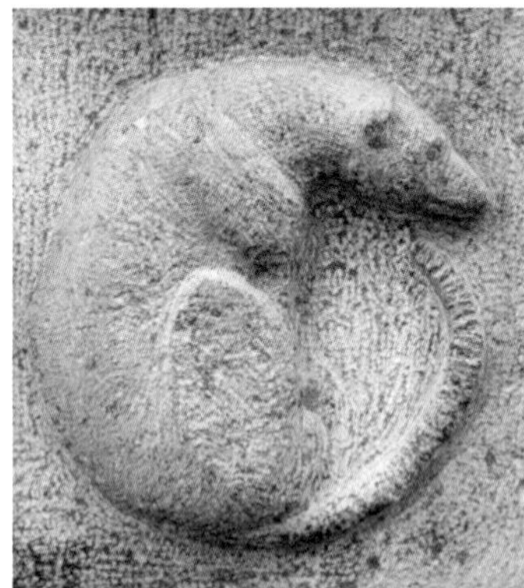

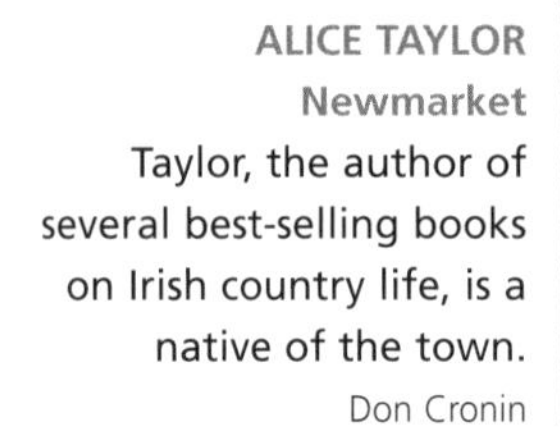

ALICE TAYLOR

Newmarket

Taylor, the author of several best-selling books on Irish country life, is a native of the town.

Don Cronin

DANCER AND FIDDLER
Lowertown, Schull
Tin dancer and fiddle-player, reminding us of when dance platforms were a place to meet to sing and dance.
Susan O'Toole

SARAH CURRAN
Newmarket
Marking one of the great love stories of Irish history: Sarah, who was the love of the patriot Robert Emmet's life, is buried here.
Don Cronin

CANON GOODMAN
Abbeystrewry Church, Bridge Street, Skibbereen
In appreciation of the legacy left by Canon Goodman, who died in 1896, for his collection of Irish music, his contribution to the Irish language and his work for the Church of Ireland in his parish.
Don Cronin

O'DONOVAN ROSSA
Memorial Garden, Skibbereen
Commemorative installation unveiled by President Michael D. Higgins in June 2015, the centenary of Rossa's death.
Architects' Dept, Cork County Council

JEREMIAH O'DONOVAN ROSSA
Entrance to O'Donovan Rossa Park, Skibbereen
The Fenian leader and member of the IRB was born in Rosscarbery in 1831 and ran a grocery shop in Skibbereen. Patrick Pearse's graveside oration at his funeral included the powerful quote: '… but the fools, the fools, the fools! They have left us our Fenian dead, and while Ireland holds these graves, Ireland unfree shall never be at peace.'
Éamon Looney

REEN FARM, UNION HALL

John Kelly

COW UP A TREE

Inspired by William Dobell's World War II papier-mâché cows and the Australian landscape, Kelly's monumental bronze sculpture was first exhibited on the Champs-Élysées in 1999 and now resides permanently in West Cork. The silence and stillness of a very foggy day combined with the iconic installations gave a surreal sense to the landscape when I took the photos.

MAQUETTE FOR PUBLIC MONUMENT

MAQUETTE FOR THREE COWS IN A PILE

ALIEN

FORM AND FUNCTION

LUNA PARK LANDSCAPE

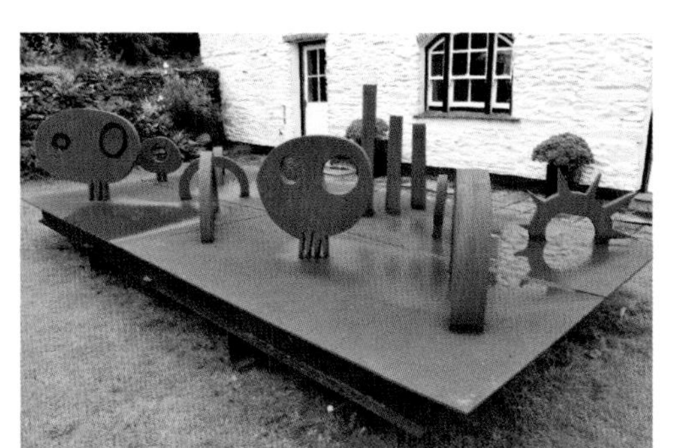

LOGO IN THE LANDSCAPE

UNTITLED
St Patrick's National School, Whitechurch
Limestone and bronze.
Mick Wilkins

BLACKWATER MOON
N25 Waterford Road roundabout, Youghal
Limestone piece representing the phases of the moon.
Alan Counihan

STONE RELIEF

Green Park, Youghal

Depicts the maritime heritage of the town.

Anthony Breslin

JOHN L. SULLIVAN
Abbeydorney
Born in 1858 and known as the Boston Strong Boy, Sullivan was recognised as the last heavyweight champion of bare-knuckle boxing under the London Prize Ring Rules and the first heavyweight champion of gloved boxing. He was also the first American athlete to win over $1m. His father was from Abbeydorney.
Kevin Holland

THE FAR-SIGHTED SCULPTOR JEROME
Tralee Road, Annascaul
The internationally renowned sculptor was born here.
Billy Leen

TOM CREAN
Annascaul
Bronze image of the iconic Antarctic explorer, who grew up here; he is shown with two puppies, a reminder of the famous photo of Tom cradling the puppies that he took care of on the ship.
Éamonn O'Doherty

BILL CLINTON
Ballybunion
The 42nd president of the United States, who has always enjoyed playing golf here.
Seán McCarthy

ENDURANCE
N86, Annascaul/Tralee road
This installation honours Tom Crean's contribution to Antarctic exploration. Aligned on a north–south axis to signify his journey from his birthplace in Annascaul to the Antarctic, the listing *Endurance* is trapped in the pack ice.
Artist's name unknown to the author

MEX I CAN
Tig Bric, Ballyferriter
A novel use of an old milk churn and pig trough, giving them a new lease of life.
Adrienne Heslin

CLIPPED WINGS
Tig Bric, Ballyferriter
A memorial piece of an angel without its wings.
Adrienne Heslin

THE FIRST BARRACKS
Gortatlea, Ballymacelligott
The piece is split to show the eruption of the attack that caused the deaths of the men commemorated on the pillar; the acorns at the centre of the blast signify renewal.
Billy Leen

SIGERSON CLIFFORD
Cahirciveen
Commemorating the poet, playwright and civil servant, who grew up in the town and is best known for his song 'The Boys of Bárr na Sráide'.
Alan Hall

EXPLORE. DREAM. DISCOVERY
St Brendan's Primary School, Blennerville
Depicts a child holding up a sail that forms a shelter for parents and children. The amphitheatre of steps reflects a boat's interior where children can sit or play.
Marjorie Cunningham

THE LADS
Cahirciveen
Joe Neeson

GATE TO THE RING OF KERRY
Cahirciveen
Gateway piece in stainless steel depicting a city gate with images of fish, seagull, bull, horse, violin, a pair of oars and a boat.
Denis O'Connor

GATEWAY PIECE
Castleisland Bypass
Artist's name unknown to the author

CHARLES HAUGHEY
Strand Street, Dingle
Bronze and limestone piece funded by Dingle fishermen in recognition of the late former taoiseach's assistance in developing the port.
Nickhola Kyle

ST BRENDAN
Cuas, at Brandon Creek
Bronze and sandstone. It is traditionally believed that Brendan departed from Cuas on his voyage in search of the promised land.
Cliodna Cussen

AN TEANGA BHEO

Pobal Scoil Corca Dhuibhne, Dingle

A large-scale abstract sculpture mounted on both faces of the spine wall at the school entrance. It weaves its way through and along the wall and is a visual interpretation of how the Irish language is interwoven into the community and how it is influenced by what is happening both inside the school and in the locality outside.

Róisín de Buitléar and Maree Hensey

PLAIN SAILING

The Mail Road, Dingle

Greenstone.

Billy Leen

SEA FORM

Boardwalk, Dingle

The spiral form suggests the slow movement of water.

Joe Neeson

PENDULUM STOPS—NINE ELEVEN

Brewery Road, Dingle

Commemorating the 9/11 attack on New York's Twin Towers.

Billy Leen

ASTROLABE

South of Dunquin ferry terminal to the Great Blasket

In memory of the sailors of the Spanish Armada who drowned in Blasket Sound in 1588. The astrolabe is a navigational instrument that was in use at the time.

Cliodna Cussen

FISHERMAN'S GATES

Farranfore

Eric O'Neill

KALEIDOSCOPE OF LIFE

Brewery Road, Dingle

A selection from a series of small stained-glass installations that can be viewed through peep-holes set in limestone display discs along the stone wall. Each panel presents an image of a different aspect of Dingle life, along with a poem written by the artist.

Mary Leen

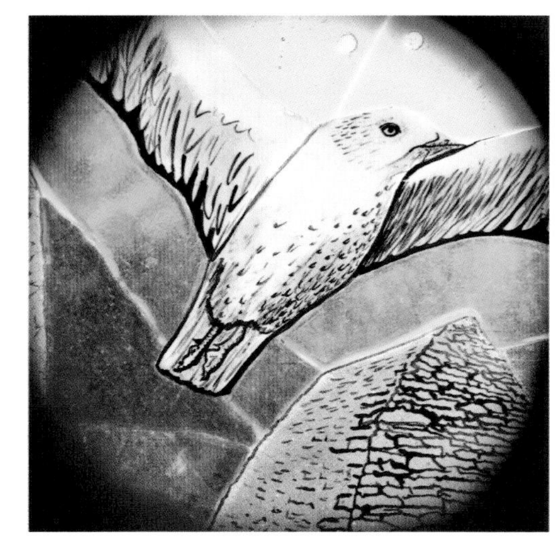

FISHERMAN
Fenit Pier

Dedicated to local fishermen, and to those whose last port was Fenit and who lost their lives to the sea.

Seamus Connolly

JOHN GOLDEN
Kells

Illuminated corten steel panel with local stone surround. Golden was involved in the failed Fenian Rising in Kells in 1867 and was deported to Australia.

Holger Lonze

NEST OF LACE
Kenmare Pier

The artist worked with residents of the Árd Bhearna Housing Estate and pupils from Pobalscoil Inbhear Scéine to design and make a bronze and stone sculpture to celebrate the tradition of lacemaking in the town. It features actual artworks created by the group and functions as a seat.

Lynn Kirkham

RUTTING STAGS
Killarney
Two bronze fighting stags.
Don Cronin

JOHNNY O'LEARY
Killarney
Bronze sculpture of the renowned traditional musician, born in Gneeveguilla in 1923. His last national achievement was a TG4 Hall of Fame award.
Mike Kenny

MONSIGNOR HUGH O'FLAHERTY
Mission Road, Killarney
Hugh O'Flaherty, known as Ireland's Oskar Schindler, was born in Kiskeam, Co. Cork, and grew up in Killarney. The 'Rome Escape Line' is credited with saving the lives of more than 6,500 people in Nazi-occupied Rome during World War II.
Alan Hall

RED DEER
New Road, Killarney
A native red deer carved from an old chestnut tree.
Will Fogarty

THE DIASPORA
Iveragh Road, Killorglin
Figure of a woman representing the Irish diaspora, carved from a 200-year-old oak tree. Project supported by Killorglin Tidy Towns Committee.
Will Fogarty and Mick Clifford

THE BALLYKISSANE TRAGEDY
Killorglin
In preparation for the 1916 Easter Rising, the IRB planned to seize a wireless to contact the German vessel *Aud*, due into Fenit with a supply of weapons on Easter Sunday. On the way to Cahirciveen on Good Friday to arrange collection of the weapons, one of the cars mistakenly took the Ballykissane road and drove off the pier, drowning four passengers. They were the first casualties of the Rising.
Alan Hall

BRYAN MACMAHON
Listowel
Commemorating the schoolteacher who was also a playwright, novelist and short-story writer.
Hugh Hanratty

JOHN B. KEANE
Listowel
The playwright and novelist lived in the town.
Seamus Connolly

MAID OF ERIN
The Square, Listowel
This rather garish stucco façade is typical of Celtic Revival 'Maid of Erin' symbols of the late nineteenth and early twentieth centuries. Erin is shown here with her harp and wolfhound, and with the rising sun and a round tower in the background. Underneath is the motto *Erin go bragh*—'Ireland forever'—which sometimes accompanied representations of Erin crafted at that time.
Patrick McAuliffe

SLÍ NA SIÓGA, THE WAY THE FAIRIES WENT
Beside the Catholic Church, Sneem
Known more commonly as the Sneem Pyramids, these stone and glass structures were created with local stoneworkers to celebrate the winning of the Tidy Towns Competition in 1987. The sculptor recalled the *síodh ghaoth*, the fairy wind that suddenly arises and vanishes again. The paths were designed to admit only a child or a fairy.
James Scanlon

DÚN AN ÓIR
Árd na Caithne, formerly Smerwick
Limestone monument commemorating the Spanish, Italian and Irish soldiers who were executed after the 1580 siege, which took place during the Desmond Rebellion.
Cliodna Cussen

THE PEACEFUL PANDA

Pier Road, Sneem

White marble panda memorial to President Cearbhall Ó Dálaigh, donated by the People's Republic of China in 1986. The president had visited China and had been an early advocate of Chinese admission to the United Nations.

CHARLES DE GAULLE

North Square, Sneem

Stone piece devoted to the memory of Charles de Gaulle, president of France 1959–69, who visited Sneem directly after his resignation as president.

Alan Hall

STEVE 'CRUSHER' CASEY

South Square, Sneem

World champion wrestler, and All-England rowing champion with his brothers. In 1982 he received the Irish Hall of Fame award.

Alan Hall

WILLIAM MULCHINOCK AND MARY O'CONNOR

The Rose Garden, Town Park, Tralee

The poet and composer William Pembroke Mulchinock with his sweetheart Mary O'Connor, who at seventeen refused his offer of marriage because she knew that she would not be accepted into his wealthy family. Broken-hearted, he went to India and became a war correspondent; when he returned six years later, in 1849, he discovered that she had died of TB a few days previously. Mary was the original Rose of Tralee.

Jeanne Rynhart

HORNS OF CLOGHERCLEMIN

Town Park, Tralee

A hoard of Bronze Age horns was found in a bog in 1875; the piece pays tribute to the craftsmanship of the ancient Irish.

Paula O'Sullivan

STANDING STONE

Town Park, Tralee

The stone is aligned with Queen Scotia's Glen on Sliabh Mis Mountain and looks back to a mythical time when the Milesians defeated the Tuatha de Danann and Scotia's son, Amergin, named the island 'Eire'.

Paula O'Sullivan

CAULDRON OF THE DAGDA
Town Park, Tralee
This bronze drinking-fountain recalls that in ancient Ireland the Dagda ('the great god') possessed one of the four treasures of the Tuatha de Danann: a vessel of endless bounty 'from which none returned unfulfilled'.
Paula O'Sullivan

SCOTIA
Scotia's Corner, Tralee
Near the spot where Scotia, the daughter of an Egyptian pharaoh, is reputed to be buried.
Billy Leen

TREE OF LEARNING
St Mary's CBS, Dan Spring Road, Tralee
Limestone.
Billy Leen

ROSE OF TRALEE
Ballymullen Roundabout, Tralee
The stone structure shows the Rose of Tralee logo and honours the community effort that goes into the organisation of the annual Rose Festival.
Billy Leen

ROSES
Tralee Bypass
Bronze.
Rory Breslin

PÁIDÍ O'SHEA
Ventry
Memorial to a great Kerry footballer.
Seamus Connolly

CIVIL WAR MEMORIAL
Ballyseedy, Tralee
Striking bronze memorial commemorating the loss of many local men in the 1922–3 Civil War.
Yann Renard Goulet

CHARLIE CHAPLIN
Seafront, Waterville
Life-size bronze of Chaplin dressed as the tramp from the 1915 film of the same name.
Alan Hall

PAYNE STEWART
Waterville Golf Club, Murreagh
Bronze statue of the famous American professional golfer who was killed in 1999 in an air crash caused by depressurisation in the plane.
Jim Connolly

ÁRTHACH DÁNA

Seafront, Waterville

In this recent impressive addition to the seafront a cold-worked bronze skin is fitted over a cantilevered stainless steel spaceframe, combining modern techniques with prehistoric metal working. Taking its inspiration from the myth of the Milesian poet Amergin and seafaring and maritime culture in prehistoric times, a boat emerges from the ground like a beached vessel from the depths of history. The elongated stem resembles the skull and beak of a Northern Gannet that becomes the gnomon of a large sundial – a reference to the Little Skellig, one of the largest gannet colonies in the world.

Holger Lonze

MICK O'DWYER

Seafront, Waterville

The Kerry All-Ireland footballer who went on to be an equally successful manager.

Alan Hall

COLONEL PAT QUINLAN

Com an Chiste viewpoint, N71 Caherdaniel/Waterville

Bronze low-relief image of the local man who commanded the Irish UN peace-keeping force in the siege of Jadotville in the Congo in 1961. Equipped with outdated weapons, 150 Irish soldiers courageously held out against 3,000 Katangese military for four days until Quinlan, without water or ammunition, had no option but to surrender to save the lives of his men. Despite having inflicted heavy casualties on the opposition, Quinlan had only five injured men.

Holger Lonze

CARVED STONE

Smugglers Inn, Waterville

Tighe O'Donoghue Ross

Limerick

CANDLE
Coláiste Íde agus Iosef, Convent Street, Abbeyfeale
Irish limestone, with the body featuring a tree of life motif, the sun, moon, stars and a centre panel from the Book of Durrow, surrounded by a design of never-ending interlacing knotwork.
R. Dennison

CARVED PLAY FEATURES
Radharc na Féile, Abbeyfeale
Limestone play features: hopscotch square and seating area, skip triangle and jump circle.
Fred Conlon

BIRDS
St Nicholas National School, Adare
Bronze on limestone: a flock of pigeons eating ivy berries.
James McCarthy

JACKIE POWER
Annacotty
The town is the birthplace of the renowned hurler.
Jim Connolly

TAKE THE BULL BY THE HORNS
Town centre, Askeaton
Stone piece.
Barry Wrafter

AHERNE BROTHERS
Athea
Known locally as 'the feet', this piece is in memory of Tim and Dan Aherne, two world-class local athletes of the early 1900s. Tim was a sprinter and hurdler, but it was in hop, step and jump—now the triple jump—that he won gold in the 1908 Olympics. He continued to win after he emigrated to the US and was awarded the Winged Foot trophy for scoring the greatest number of points for the New York Athletic Club. Dan set a record for the hop, step and jump that remained unbeaten for years; he emigrated in 1908 and over the next twelve years he won eight American championships.
Jim Flavin

THE GARDENS

The Gardens Housing Estate, Ballingarry

A selection from a collection of motifs on sandstone planter boxes at each side of a paved area.

Martha Quinn

DAIBHÍ Ó BRÚADAIR MEMORIAL

Broadford

Bronze piece commemorating the significant seventeenth-century Irish-language poet.

Cliodna Cussen

MURALS
Bruff
Neil O'Dwyer

JOHN 'THE BULL' HAYES
The great Cappamore rugby player who retired in 2011.

Commemorating the Flight of the Earls in 1607.

Racing mural honouring the Limerick racehorse owner J.P. McManus.

REFLECTION
Library, Cappamore
Commemorative piece of a bouquet of lilies in forged steel. The cut flowers signify the lives of all ages cut short by the 1916 Easter Rising, and the folds of the material in the inscription plate reflect the delicacy of a parchment, paying tribute to the Proclamation document.
Eric O'Neill

FAMINE MEMORIAL
St Michael's Church, Cappamore
Bronze plaque depicting a starving homeless family resting on the roadside, commemorating those of the area who died in the Famine. It is accompanied by a quote from the poet Padraic Colum: 'A plague wind blew across the land, fever was in the air; fields were black that once were green and death was everywhere'.
Michael Killen

A BENCH FOR THE BULL
Library, Cappamore
Dedicated to rugby player John 'the Bull' Hayes.
Eric O'Neill

MUNSTER GATES
Cappamore
The design pays tribute to Munster rugby.
Eric O'Neill

MICK MACKEY
Castle Street, Castleconnell
The triple All-Ireland-winning hurler, recognised as one of the sport's greats.
Seamus Connolly

WOMAN AND CHILD
Ash Crescent, Croom
Barry Wrafter.

BIRD STONE
Towerfield, Croom
Stainless steel bird sculpture.
Marie Brett

BOY ON A BALL
The Fort Housing Estate, Doon
Artist's name unknown to the author

THREE MARTYRS MEMORIAL
Chrochta, Kilmallock
Commemorating a bishop and two priests who were tortured and hanged here in the late sixteenth century.
Cliodna Cussen

STAKER WALLACE
Town centre, Kilfinnane
After Wallace's involvement in the 1798 Rebellion he was flogged, hanged, drawn and quartered, and his head displayed on a pike.
Cliodna Cussen

THE CHASE
Ballyea Close, Fedamore
A dog and cat in Irish cut limestone.
Barry Wrafter

LOUGH GUR MARKERS

Lough Gur

A selection from five markers in corten steel and bronze on the lakeside walk.

Deiseal

TERRY WOGAN

Harvey's Quay, Limerick

The famous radio and television personality was born in Limerick.

Rory Breslin

DOCKERS MONUMENT
Spokane Walk, Limerick City
Bronze piece honouring the men, including the artist's father, who worked on the city's docks.
Michael Duhan

TREE SCULPTURE
People's Park, Pery Square, Limerick
Three little dogs carved on the base of a dead tree, appropriately sited in a park where there is much dog-walking activity.
Will Fogarty

RICHARD HARRIS
Bedford Row, Limerick
The actor is shown in the role of King Arthur in *Camelot.*
Jim Connolly

MICHAEL HOGAN
King John's Castle, Limerick
Life-size bronze of the nineteenth-century poet known as the Bard of Thomond.
Jim Connolly

ANTHONY FOLEY
Clancy's Strand, Thomond Park, Limerick
Limestone memorial stone engraved with an image of 'Axel' charging forward with the ball.
Colin Grehan, with Irish Natural Stone

ÚLL ORGA / GOLDEN APPLE
St Nessan's Community College, Moylish Park, Limerick
Rachel Joynt

TO THE PEOPLE OF LIMERICK
Southern Ring Road, Limerick
Cylinder of stick people, one standing on the other, symbolising the people of Limerick: without the people there is no city, and without the stick people there is no structure.
Kevin McMahon

SHANNON FLEET I
Limerick tunnel and M7, Annaholty Section
A series of high concrete and steel longship prows and corten steel heads celebrating the historic presence of Vikings on the Shannon.
Deiseal

IRISH ELK
Coonagh Roundabout, Limerick
Artist's name unknown to the author

SHANNON FLEET II
N7 Limerick Bypass, Clare side of Limerick Tunnel
Deiseal

JOHN FLANAGAN
Martinstown
The world champion hammer-thrower emigrated in 1897 and joined the New York police. He won gold in the Olympics of 1900, 1904 and 1908.
Jeanne Rynhart

FIOS
St Nessan's National School, Mungret
Cast bronze and sheet bronze, inspired by the shape of an Early Christian bell. The upper third takes the form of a ram; the lower two thirds are like pages of a book and are inscribed with the stories of the three Fionns and the Salmon of Knowledge, St Nessan and the ram, and a quote from *Auraicept na nEces.*
Niall O'Neill

UNIVERSITY OF LIMERICK

PHOENIX
Robert Schuman Building
Stainless steel.
Alexandra Wejchert

NICHE
University of Limerick plaza
Bronze and corten steel figure with bowed head and outstretched arms. Two golden trees grow from the back of the hands. The piece is about a desire for personal growth and self-discovery. The figure towers above university life, drawing on inner strengths to seek equilibrium and find one's niche.
Orla de Brí

SILVER PENCILS
Reflecting pool, Foundation Building
Kinetic sculpture; polished aluminium with stainless steel shafts.
Peter Logan

DR PAUL QUIGLEY
Quigley Building
Michael McTigue

TOTEM POLE
Abbeyowney, Murroe
Bronze and stone depicting spheres of different shapes being compressed with the attributes of a totem pole.
Barry Wrafter

CAILÍN DEAS CRÚITE NA MBÓ
Town Square, Newcastlewest
In the 1950s a cross was installed on this site to mark the Marian Year and the Latin inscription associated with it is still visible on the plinth. Now it is home to a buttermaid holding her butterpat, milk churns and a mill-wheel, in recognition of the significance of the dairy industry in the area.
Cliodna Cussen

MICHAEL HARTNETT
Town Square, Newcastlewest
Bronze figure on limestone of the bilingual poet who was born locally.
Rory Breslin

SOPHIE PEIRCE PLAQUE
Town Square, Newcastlewest
The amazing adventurer known as 'the flying Irishwoman' was born in Newcastlewest, and when she died in 1939 her ashes were scattered over the town.
Cliodna Cussen

NUMBER PLATES, STREET SIGNS
Ash Crescent, Oak Crescent, Sycamore Crescent, Newcastlewest
Two of a series of decorative bronze number plates and street signs spread around the estate.
Marie Brett

PADDY RYAN
Pallasgreen
World record-holder and Olympic gold and silver medallist in hammer-throwing.
Seamus Connolly

THE ONE THAT GOT AWAY
Near the church, Rathkeale
Kilkenny limestone butcher holding a piglet. Even though it has, regrettably, suffered damage in several parts since installation (mainly the butcher's hat and nose, and the ears of both butcher and pig), I include it because I found it a very engaging piece.
Barry Wrafter

Tipperary

FISH ABOUNDING
Cahir
A leaping salmon in bronze, depicting Cahir's centuries-old link with fishing. The town's ancient name is *Cathair-Dúna-Iascaigh*, 'fort of the fortification abounding in fish'.
Jarlath Daly

MAURICE DAVIN
Clonmel Road, Carrick-on-Suir
Davin was co-founder with Michael Cusack of the Gaelic Athletic Association, and its first president.
Barry Wrafter

SETTLEMENT
M8 Cashel/Mitchelstown Bypass, Exit 10
The ruin of a small house in a meadow beside the motorway exit. With broad windows and smooth surface, the lower part of the building reflects an average contemporary house, but the rendering blends into natural stone that is rough and weathered near the top, and it begins to look like a ruin.
Cornelia Konrads

HISTORY IN STONE

Seán Healy Park, Carrick-on-Suir

A selection from eleven limestone standing stones that tell the story of the town in words and carvings. The inscriptions are based on the poetic work 'All Souls' by local poet Michael Coady.

Tony O'Malley

VINCENT O'BRIEN
Rosegreen Village, Cashel
Figure of the great horse-trainer.
Artist's name unknown to the author

NOTHING ODD WILL DO LONG
The Quay, Clonmel
Commemorative piece comprising four limestone columns; three pieces have bronze plaques on top and when viewed through a small hole in the first column the plaques align to form the face of novelist and Anglican clergyman Laurence Sterne, who was born in the town in 1713.
Ron Van der Noll

THOMAS MacDONAGH
Cloughjordan

Bronze figure showing teacher and poet MacDonagh, a native of the town. He was one of the signatories of the Proclamation of the Irish Republic and was executed following the 1916 Easter Rising. He is depicted holding the Proclamation, and viewers can stand beside the statue and read the document.

Mark Rode

TREE
Scoil Chrónáin Naofa, Dromakeenan

Paul Finch

THE THREE OLYMPIANS
Courthouse, Ashe Road, Nenagh

Bronze piece honouring Olympic athletes Johnny Hayes, Matt McGrath and Bob Tisdall, all of whom had Nenagh roots.

Jeanne Rynhart

LANNAN'S FAREWELL
Nenagh
Mural inspired by the song 'Lannan's Farewell to Nenagh', attributed to John Kelly, from the late 1800s, and a photo of traditional musician John Doherty taken in 1974 by American photographer Jill Freedman.
Dermot McConaghy

TREE OF LIFE
Gortnataggart Housing Estate, Thurles
The artist worked with residents of the housing estate to design and make a large bronze for the estate entrance. It features the actual artworks created by the group and is a popular meeting place.
Lynn Kirkham

AG DUL GO DTÍ AN AONACH / GOING TO THE FAIR
Teach an Léinn, Kenyon Street, Nenagh
Two scrap-metal cows mounted on the wall of the building near the railway station.
Lynn Kirkham and Paul Finch

THE DANDELION
Rathnaveogue M7, north of Moneygall
A girl blowing a dandelion carved into a large slab, giving the idea that the clocks blown from the plant are taken further on their journey by the passing vehicles.
Michael Disley

IT'S A LONG WAY TO TIPPERARY
Market Place, Tipperary Town
Steel sculpture mounted on a large piece of local limestone. Inspired by the compass rose, a symbol of distance, journeys and adventure, and believed to bring good luck and protection to travellers.
Lynn Kirkham

THE OLD HURLEY-MAKER

Parnell Street, Thurles

Mural of a hurley-maker in the town that was the birthplace of the GAA.

Neil O'Dwyer

Waterford

FISHERMAN
Seafront, Ardmore
John Hayes

MASTER McGRATH
Junction
Clonmel/Cappoquin roads
Born in Dungarvan in 1866, this was the country's most celebrated greyhound.
Artist's name unknown to author

ICE, FIRE AND WATER
Copper Coast Geopark
Represents the common forces that shaped the Copper Coast and its European Geoparks partners in north-west Europe.

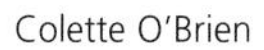

Colette O'Brien

BLUE FORM
Causeway, Dungarvan
Artist's name unknown to the author

DAILY BALANCE
The Plaza, Dungarvan
Limestone piece of a man with a churn, on the site of the former creamery.
Patrick Barry

REGENERATION AND SOULS OF THE SEA
The Harbour, Dunmore East
Bronze piece commissioned by the people of Dunmore East, with a list of names of those lost in local waters.
Pat Cunningham and John O'Connor

MURAL
Dunmore East
Building frontage.
Art by Eoin

THE SINGING HAT
Dunmore East
Elaborate musical-themed carving on a large tree stump beside the Haven Hotel. It includes a guitar, a banjo, piano keys, music symbols and a man with a bodhran.
John Hayes

THE HOLY TREE
Church of the Immaculate Conception, Fenor
Carved Monterey pine tree in the graveyard.
John Hayes

Convent Street, Tallow
Three plaques on a wall:

TOBIAS KIRBY
Tobias Kirby was appointed rector of the Irish College in Rome in 1849.
James McCarthy

FRANK RYAN
Low-relief bronze portrait of the famous Irish tenor of the 1940s and 1950s.
James McCarthy

JOHN HOGAN
One of Ireland's greatest sculptors, who died in 1858, was born in Tallow.
Artist's name unknown to the author

WATERFORD WALLS, TRAMORE

HERON
Strand Road
Dan Leo

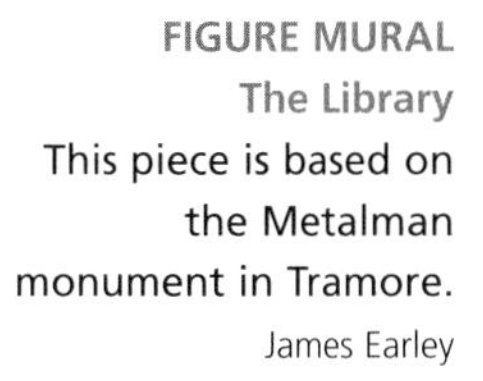

FIGURE MURAL
The Library
This piece is based on the Metalman monument in Tramore.
James Earley

PROMENADHA
Main Street
Dermot McConaghy

PAINTED BUILDING
Building frontage
Art by Eoin

NED POWER
Tallow
Tribute to the great Dungarvan-born All-Ireland-winning hurler.
Seán McCarthy

HORSES
Convent Street, Tallow
The town has a large annual horse fair, founded in 1910.
Artist's name unknown to the author

UNTITLED
The Quays, Waterford
A tall, maritime-inspired piece in laminated larch commemorating the Wallace brothers, musicians and composers.
Eithne Ring and Liam Lavery

BOAT
The Quays, Waterford
Stainless steel.
Denis O'Connor

STRONGBOW AND AOIFE
Bishop's Palace Garden, Waterford
Bronze figures marking the most important marriage in Irish history.
Eithne Ring and Liam Lavery

FINAL JOURNEY
The Quays, Waterford
Denis O'Connor

CONDON MEMORIAL
Cathedral Square, Waterford
In memory of the men, women and children of Waterford who lost their lives as a result of armed conflict at home and abroad. John Condon, born in Waterford, is long believed to have been the youngest Allied soldier killed in WWI—aged fourteen, as shown on his gravestone.
Pat Cunningham

LUKE WADDING
Greyfriars, Waterford
Franciscan friar who founded the Irish College in Rome.
Gabriel Hayes

THE MEETING OF THE HANDS
Canada Street, Waterford
Artist's name unknown to the author

LEGACY
Presentation College, Cannon Street, Waterford
The shape of this bronze sculpture references the conical turrets in Pugin's convent and school buildings.
Barry Linnane

WATERFORD WALLS, WATERFORD CITY

SEE NO EVIL, HEAR NO EVIL, SPEAK NO EVIL
Michael Street
The model for the monkey poses is the artist's brother Alfie.
Caoilfhionn Hanton

BULL
New Street
Represents the bull of Celtic mythology.
James Earley

IN THE WOODSSS
New Street Gardens
Two unlikely friends who forged a bond because of their common interest in hip hop.
Niall O'Lochlainn

TIGER
Saving animals through street art.
Sonny

TORBE 36
Apple Market
The young Mexican painter opens a window between two continents.
Mantra

AR SCATH A CHÉILE A MHAIREANN NA DAOINE
Former Árd na Rí hotel
The title translates as 'We live protected under each other's shadow'. The artist wanted people to find hope when they looked up at the mural. It is installed to confront stigma, to question how we find our moral compass and to challenge us to build resilience, but above all it is a symbol of support. It followed the opening in the city of Pieta House, the suicide and self-harm crisis organisation.
Joe Caslin

Ulster

Antrim

CHILDREN OF LIR
Seafront, Ballycastle
Representing the legend of the four children who were turned into swans by their jealous stepmother, and condemned to spend 300 years on Lake Derravarragh, 300 on the Straits of Moyle and 300 at Inishglora (near Erris, Co. Mayo).
Malcolm Robertson

BUTTERFLY WALL
Broughshane, Ballymena
Kris Copeland and Ross Wilson, with local children

LEAP OF FAITH
The Harbour, Ballycastle
Malcolm Robertson

BIRD'S NEST AND EGGS
Broughshane riverside walk, Ballymena
Donnacha Cahill

APPLES
People's Park, Ballymena
Each apple represents a historically significant period. The artist associates the symbolism of the apple with Adam and Eve, William Tell, Isaac Newton and Steve Jobs. Collectively the apples symbolise some community-based themes: working together, trust, growth and peace-building.
Shiro Masuyama

JOEY AND ROBERT DUNLOP
Ballymoney
Memorial garden dedicated to the great motor-cycling brothers. Joey was killed in a race in Tallinn in 2000, and Robert in a practice run for the North West 200 in 2008. Tragically for the Dunlop family, while this book was in preparation Robert's son William was killed in a crash in Dublin in July 2018.
Amanda Barton

SPIRIT OF BELFAST
Arthur Square, Belfast
Four curved stainless steel structures installed on a granite base.
Dan George

REGENERATION
Blackstaff Square, Belfast
Bronze and fibreglass chrysalis-to-butterfly piece symbolising the regeneration of the city.
Anna Cheyne

ALEC THE GOOSE
St George's Market, Belfast
This goose, owned by a local poultry vendor, was a favourite in the area and a regular visitor to the market during the 1920s.
Gordon Muir

CARRAIG FÁILTE / WELCOME STONE
Junction of Monagh Road/Upper Springfield Road, Turf Lodge, Belfast
A free-standing Celtic ogham stone with bronze plates.
Farhad Nargol O'Neill

CARRAIG MAIGHRÉAD / MARGARET'S STONE
Entrance to Áit na Móna Estate, Monagh Bypass, Belfast
Farhad Nargol O'Neill

THE SPIRIT OF HEDGE AND HOUND
Falls Park, Falls Road, Belfast
Stainless steel hunting dog referencing the history of the park—originally a deer-park belonging to the Donegall estate which was used for hunting with dogs. A walking trail of steel pawprints leads from the sculpture around the park.
Martin Heron

JAMES CONNOLLY
Falls Road, Belfast
Born in Scotland to Irish parents, Connolly was the founder of the Irish Citizen Army and was sentenced to death by firing squad for his part in the 1916 Easter Rising. Having been badly injured in the conflict, he was taken to his execution by stretcher and was shot strapped to a chair. Michael Collins said of him that he 'would have followed him through hell'.
Steve Feeny

FORGET ME NOT
Belfast City Cemetery, Falls Road
Bronze-coated stainless steel commemorative piece, commissioned under the Building Peace Through the Arts initiative for the unmarked mass graves. The design and position of the piece invite us to contemplate the unborn, the young and the old who have been laid to rest in the surrounding unmarked plots. Forget-me-not flowers and buds are used to symbolise the fragility and diversity of life.
Alex Pentek

THE BOXER
Woodvale Park, Shankill, Belfast
Bronze figure celebrating the boxing tradition in the area.
Mark Richards

JOHN CALDWELL
Dunville Park, Belfast
Commemorating the flyweight boxer who won bronze at the Melbourne Olympic Games in 1956.
Alan Beattie Herriott

CONOR'S CORNER
Shankill Road/Northumberland Street corner, Belfast
Commemorating the painter William Conor.
Holger Lonze

RINTY MONAGHAN
Buoy Park, Cathedral Gardens, Belfast
Commemorating the local flyweight boxing hero of the 1940s.
Alan Beattie Herriott

THE FLYING ANGEL

Princes Dock Street, Belfast

The flying angel is a worldwide symbol of the Seafarers' Mission, set up by an Anglican clergyman in the nineteenth century to provide care for sailors. This angel is in the act of calming the waves.

Maurice Harron

TITANICA

Titanic Exhibition Centre, Belfast

Symbolising hope and positive renewal.

Rowan Gillespie

PENNY FOR YOUR THOUGHTS

Gordon Street, Exchange Place, Belfast

An interpretation of the role of commerce in the city's development.

Peter Rooney

KIT

Titanic Quarter, Belfast

Bronze 'airfix' model of the *Titanic* beside the Abercorn Basin, near where the real ship was launched in 1911. The giant modelling kit uses scale replicas of the ship's component parts.

Tony Stallard

INDUSTRIAL HOMAGE

Newtownards Road, Belfast

Corten steel cut into shapes reminiscent of ships' hulls, celebrating the industrial heritage of the area.

Ned Jackson Smyth

LET'S TWIST AGAIN

City East Enterprise Park, Belfast

Rolled and fabricated steel, illustrating the industrial heritage of the area, including shipbuilding, ropeworks and the linen industry.

Malcolm Robertston

YARDMEN

Dr Pitt Memorial Park, Newtownards Road, Belfast

Three bronze shipyard workers walking home from Harland & Wolff, where the *Titanic* was built. In the background are the two shipbuilding gantry cranes at Queen's Island. Known as Samson and Goliath, these mighty structures dominate the city's skyline.

Ross Wilson

THE SEARCHER

Holywood Arches Library, Holywood Road, Belfast

C.S. Lewis centenary sculpture based on the character of Digory Kirke from the Narnia story. In *The Magician's Nephew* it was Digory who made the wardrobe from a beautiful apple tree that had magical properties and helped open a doorway to Narnia.

Ross Wilson

YOGA

C.S. Lewis Square, Belfast

This smiling girl is encouraging us to keep fit.

Michael Disley

NARNIA

C.S. Lewis Square, Newtownards Road, Belfast

Sculptures of bronze, cast stainless steel, cast bronze, plate stainless steel, plate bronze and granite relating to *The Chronicles of Narnia*, the seven fantasy novels by Lewis that are classics of children's literature.

Maurice Harron

TUMNUS
THE FAUN

MR AND MRS BEAVER

ASLAN THE GREAT LION

QUEEN JADIS
THE WHITE WITCH

MAUGRIM THE POWERFUL WOLF

MOTHER DAUGHTER SISTER
Sandy Row, Belfast
Celebrating the female culture and identity of Sandy Row and the contribution that women in the area have made to both family and workplace.
Ross Wilson

DAME MARY PETERS
Mary Peters Track, Malone Road, Belfast
Bronze figure of the women's pentathlon gold medal-winner at the Munich Olympics in 1972. She also represented Northern Ireland at every Commonwealth Games from 1958 to 1974, winning two gold medals for the pentathlon and gold and silver for the shot putt.
John Sherlock

RISE
Broadway Roundabout, Westlink, Belfast
The largest piece of public sculpture in the city and visible for miles, the two globes, cast in silver and white steel, seem to hover above the interchange and are lit to symbolise the rising of the sun and new hope for the city's future.
Wolfgang Buttress

CREATURE

Malone House, Barnetts Demesne, Belfast

Small bronze of a shy little animal hiding under some oak leaves, with the quotation 'Thou grimmest far o' grusome tykes. Grubbin thy food by thorny dykes' from 'To a Hedgehog' by Samuel Thompson.

Amanda Montgomery

LOSS
Malone House, Barnetts Demesne, Malone Road, Belfast

Jane Mortimer

AEROBICS
Knockbreda Centre, Saintfield Road, Belfast

Michael Disley

THE THREE GARDENERS

Musgrave Park Hospital, Stockman's Lane, Belfast

Sited at the Acquired Brain Injury Unit of the hospital, the three pieces are carved in Derbyshire gritstone. It was the artist's hope that these cheerful little figures would lift the spirits of the viewers.

Michael Disley

THE HAPPY APPLE

Based on an Irish nursery rhyme that begins 'If I were an apple and grew upon a tree, I think I'd fall down on a nice boy like me'.

AS THIN AS A RAKE

Depicts a portly gardener hiding behind a rake.

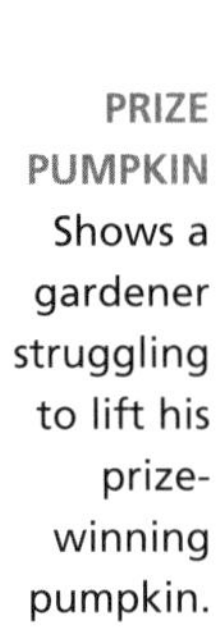

PRIZE PUMPKIN

Shows a gardener struggling to lift his prize-winning pumpkin.

GENESIS

Knockbracken Brain Injury Unit, Belfast

Jane Mortimer

THE SEAHORSE
Dargan Road, Belfast
Commissioned to record the 400th anniversary of the first quay to be constructed in the city, on High Street in 1613. The piece has a strong connection to Belfast's origins: in the seventeenth century the city's first merchants printed seahorses on their coins, and there are two seahorses on the city's coat of arms.
Ralf Sander

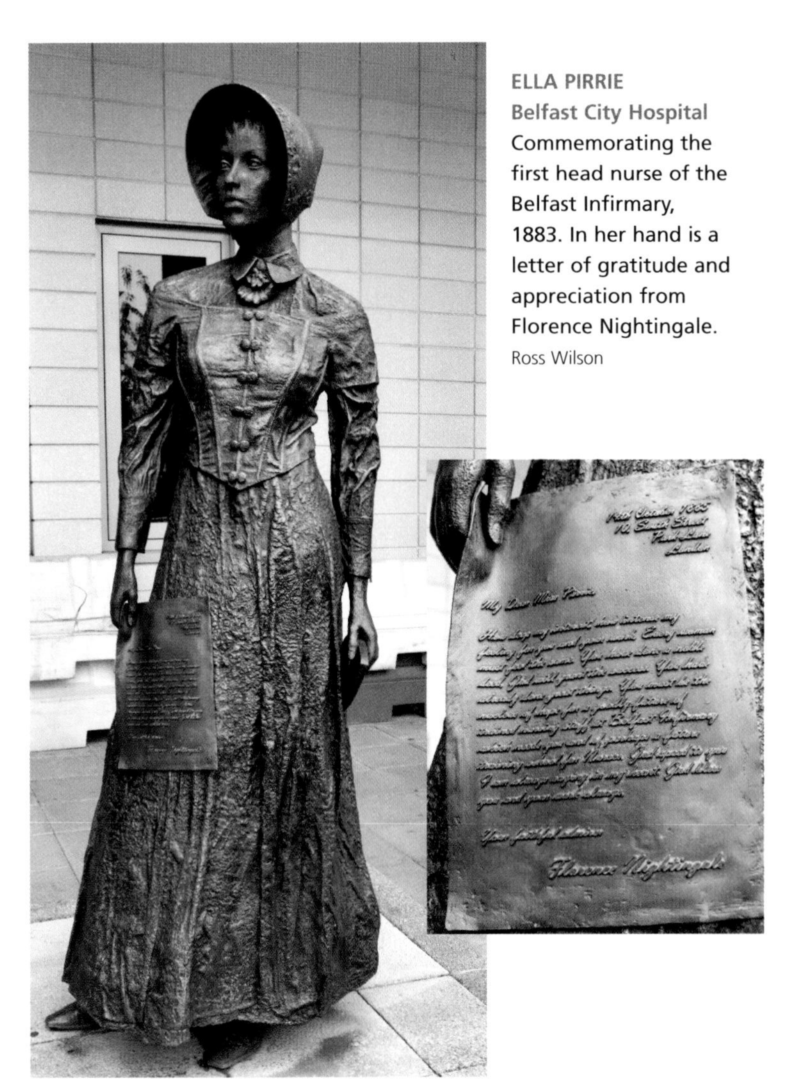

ELLA PIRRIE
Belfast City Hospital
Commemorating the first head nurse of the Belfast Infirmary, 1883. In her hand is a letter of gratitude and appreciation from Florence Nightingale.
Ross Wilson

MORE THAN A FLIGHT OF FANCY
Mill Avenue, Ligoniel Road, Belfast
Three stainless steel mallard ducks on an arch of flax flowers soaring above the historic flax dams, celebrating the history of the linen industry of the Ligoniel Dams.
Eleanor Wheeler and Alan Cargo

QUEEN'S UNIVERSITY BELFAST

ECO

The Library

In celebration of the centenary of Queen's University and the opening of the new library.

Marc Didou

RECLINING FIGURE

Lanyon Building

F.E. McWilliam

SUSTRANS

Carnlough

One of a series of installations for the Sustrans Cycle Network.

Niall Walsh

SGT ROBERT QUIGG
Town centre, Bushmills
Unveiled by Queen Elizabeth in 2016. She had met this soldier on her coronation tour in 1953.
David Annand

WATERS OF THE RIVER BUSH
Hamill Terrace, Bushmills
A fountain piece.
Holger Lonze

THE ALPHABET ANGEL
Dunarave Park, Bushmills
The bronze alphabet man celebrates the Ulster Scots dialect, which is part of life in the village.
Ross Wilson

LITTLE ACORNS
Roundabout on Greystone Road, off M2
Powder-coated steel and stainless steel oak tree, each leaf of which was designed by a member of the local community.
Alan Cargo

HERON
Loughshore Park, Jordanstown
Inspired by the local seascape of Belfast Lough and the start of the Causeway Coastal Route.
Elizabeth O'Kane

SHORELINES
Loughshore Park, Jordanstown
Bronze and stainless steel piece commissioned to mark the start of the Causeway Coastal Route, a road that follows the coastline north as far as Mussenden Temple.
Chris Wilson

SHELL
Loughshore Park, Jordanstown
A small, delicate bronze inspired by the twisting action needed to spin the threads, cords and ropes manufactured at the local linen mills. Making different grades of cord required thinning and refinement; shells also have a gradation along their length, as the spiralling gets finer towards the point. Real linen materials were used to create the effect.
Lara Greene

THE CROWN
Circular Road Roundabout, Larne
Installed to mark Queen Elizabeth's diamond jubilee in 2012.
Larne Skills Development

THE STERN
Harbour Roundabout, Larne
Steel ship's stern designed as a welcome to people arriving on the ferry from Scotland.
Paul Hogarth Company

UDR MEMORIAL
Town Square, Lisburn
A soldier and greenfinch commemorating the service of the UDR to Ulster.
John Sherlock

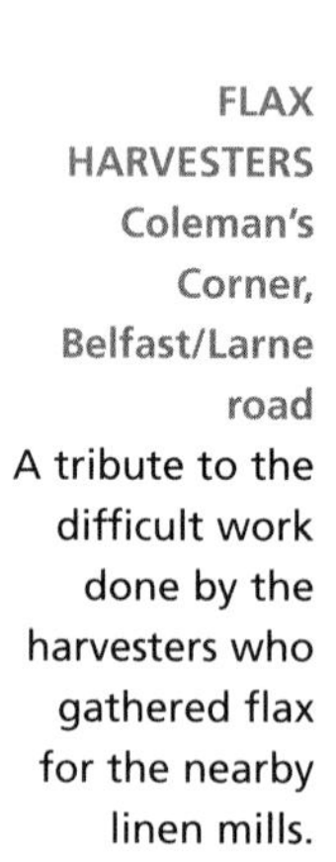

FLAX HARVESTERS
Coleman's Corner, Belfast/Larne road
A tribute to the difficult work done by the harvesters who gathered flax for the nearby linen mills.
Skelton Rainey

RESCUE
Fire & Rescue Service HQ, Seymour Street, Lisburn
This bronze sculpture of a fireman rescuing a child pays tribute to the work of the Northern Ireland Fire Service.
Maurice Harron

IF YOU GET LOST
Laganbank Road roundabout, Lisburn
Corten steel needle and thread representing the town's linen industry. A stainless steel thread through the needle's eye forms the words 'if you get lost just stop and ask for directions'. The text came from discussions with local community groups about their sense of place and identity.
Martin Heron

PROFESSOR FRANK PANTRIDGE
Island Centre, Lisburn
Physician, cardiologist and pioneer of the mobile defibrillator and coronary care.
John Sherlock

BOXING HARES
Mosside
'The hare is never inactive and serves as an example of discreet productive activity and survival, which reaches beyond the first knowledge of man in North Antrim.'
Ross Wilson

DAMASK CONTINUOUS PROFILE
Hillhall Road/Ballentine Gardens roundabout, Lisburn
Galvanised plate damask image celebrating the history of the linen industry in the area.
Ngaire Jackson and Clare Lawson

GREYHOUND
Mosside
Ross Wilson

THEATRE AT THE MILL, MOSSLEY MILL, NEWTOWNABBEY

THREADS OF TIME

Bronze piece celebrating the history of Mossley linen mill—a table with a damask linen cloth that transforms into a landscape depicting the geography of the area. A museum dedicated to the linen mill is also located here.

Chris Wilson

TALKING TREE

The stainless steel rowan tree is a community-based Peace III-funded project. The artist weaved the story of the local community together to tell the story of 'what Newtownabbey means to me …' in their own words.

Kevin Killen

FLAX FLOWER

Bronze piece paying homage to the heritage of the site, which owes much of its past to this indigenous plant.

Alan Burke

TO THE PEOPLE OF THE SEA
East Strand, Portrush
Sheet bronze and stainless steel, the three sails of a traditional drontheim morph into the surface of the sea.
Holger Lonze

MOTHER IRELAND
Shane's Castle, Randalstown
White marble piece near the dramatic castle ruins on the shore of Lough Neagh, where some filming of the *Game of Thrones* series took place. Commissioned by Lord and Lady O'Neill in memory of their son who died in WWI, it represents the figure of Ireland mourning her sons killed in battle. The private estate is open to the public for certain functions each year.
A.J. Victor Segoffin

PIPER AND DANCER
Portglenone
Known locally as Piper Sam and Irish dancer Roisin.
Billy McCaughern

Armagh

GARGOYLES AND ANGELS

Armagh City

A selection from a miniature sculpture trail of over twenty tiny gargoyles and angels who escaped the city's cathedrals in June 2010 and are now roaming the streets. Cast in bronze using sustainable Bronze Age methods, these appealing little creatures are located across a range of city centre locations—map available from the tourist office.

Holger Lonze

McCrumm's Court, wall

Uluru Restaurant, Market Street, window ledge

AMMA Centre, Market Place, ground level

6 Russell Street, on high ledge

Bank of Ireland, Upper English Street, at shoe scraper

Trimprint, 36 Upper English Street, ledge

Charlemont Hotel, Upper English Street, high on wall

Catholic cathedral,
front fence pillar

Public Library, wall beside it

5 Castle Street, top of wall
opposite house

Gas Lamp Pub, Thomas Street,
at lamp

Butter Market, Dobbin Street, beside clock

34 Scotch Street, climbing
the gable wall

Northern Bank, Scotch Street,
overlooking ATM machine

TURNING POINT
The Mall, Armagh
Bronze globe supported by four figures in the form of negative life-casts. It is possible to look through the eyeholes of each one and their positive aspects can be viewed in the interior space.
Robert Connolly

ARMAGH RAIL DISASTER
The Mall, Armagh
Bronze and limestone piece commemorating an 1889 rail disaster, when a packed Sunday School excursion train stalled while attempting to negotiate a steep incline and the rear portion rolled back down, colliding with a following train. Eighty people were killed and 260 injured, about a third of them children.
Rory Breslin

BRIAN BORU
St Patrick's Cathedral Gardens, Armagh
Bronze head on limestone base of the high-king of Ireland who was killed in the Battle of Clontarf in 1014.
Rory Breslin

CÚCHULAINN CHALLENGES YOUR ARRIVAL
Navan Centre and Fort, Killylea Road, Armagh
Willow-work piece of the mythological hero of the battle against Queen Medbh in the *Táin Bó Cúailnge.*
Heather McDermott

FLAX FLOWER
The Pond, Bessbrook
The Camlough River was harnessed at Bessbrook Pond to power the mill that drove the local economy. The key to this industry was the flax plant.
Alan Burke

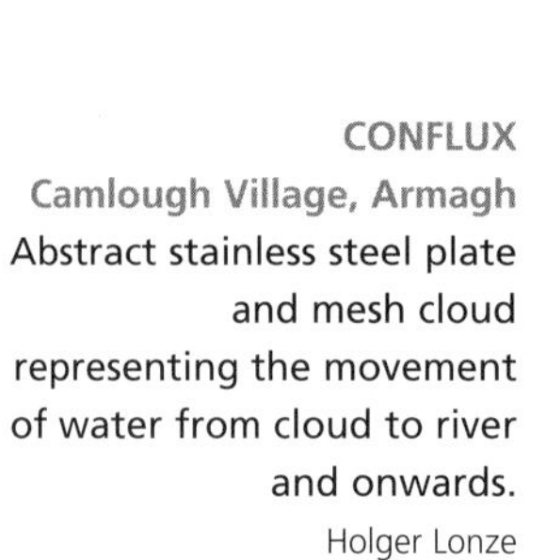

CONFLUX
Camlough Village, Armagh
Abstract stainless steel plate and mesh cloud representing the movement of water from cloud to river and onwards.
Holger Lonze

LINEN BLEACHERS
High Street, Lurgan
Figures of a man and woman, depicting the linen trade.
Maurice Harron

MASTER McGRATH
High Street, Lurgan
Ireland's most famous racing greyhound—winner of the Waterloo Cup in 1868, 1869 and 1871. When he died of heart disease in 1873, an autopsy revealed that his heart was unusually large—twice the size of a normal dog's—and was thought to be the reason for his success. He is buried in Lurgan.
Artist's name unknown to the author

WINGS
Kinnego Marina, Lurgan
Powder-coated and painted steel piece based on the traditional spritsails of the Lough Neagh fishing-boats. It is situated on the outer breakwater and serves as a navigational marker for the marina.
Holger Lonze

THE NAVIGATORS
Maghery village, Lough Neagh
Two bronze figures holding oars; the piece explores boating and fishing traditions on Lough Neagh.
Holger Lonze

THE CALLIAGH BÉARA
Slieve Gullion Forest Park, Meigh
This piece follows the footsteps of the legendary Fionn MacCumhaill of the Fianna and the myth of Fionn finding a beautiful woman crying at the water's edge.
Eleanor Wheeler

REBUILDING THE WORLD
West Street/Northway, Portadown
Three figures holding segments of an apple, reflecting the influence of the apple industry in the area.
Maurice Harron

WAVES
Oxford Island Nature Reserve, Lough Neagh
Artist's name unknown to the author

HUMAN SUNDIAL
Oxford Island Nature Reserve, Lough Neagh
There are detailed instructions, in case the sun is shining!
Jonathan Kerr

Cavan

PLEDGE OF THE METALMEN

Market House, Bailieborough

The image of two men pouring molten metal reflects the industrial heritage of the town and acknowledges the work of the men in the Bailieborough Foundry.

Barry Linnane

VILLAGE SIGN

Ballyhaise

Carved wooden signpost.

Joey Burns

THE CROSSING POINT

Market Square, Ballyconnell

Large steel water sculpture with a carved stone 'bridge' top, mounted on a circular paved area with semicircular bench seating. A project designed to promote peace and integration in the Ballyconnell area.

Tim Ward

PERCY FRENCH
Main Square, Ballyjamesduff
Percy French graduated as a civil engineer from Trinity College in 1881 and joined the Board of Works. He was a painter, poet, entertainer and composer of many well-known songs.
Alan Hall

OPES AND ECHOES OF FORM
Town Hall Street, Cavan
The work is a reflection of the architectural heritage of the town. The piece has mirrored window-like openings that reflect light and provide a contrast to the monolithic upright forms. The project involved community arts workshops where local people contributed to the text that wraps around the piece.
Fiona Murphy

THE FOUNTAIN HEADS
Main Street, Cavan
Niall O'Neill

DANCE, DANCE, WHEREVER YOU MAY BE
Town Hall Street, Cavan
Tina Quinn

FAUGH A BALLAGH
Con Smith Park, Cathedral Road, Cavan
Two figures commemorating those who died in World War I.
Tina Quinn

THE BIG ONE
Cavan Institute of Technology, Cathedral Road, Cavan
Abstract version of a Celtic cross.
Barry Wrafter

FIDDLE HEAD
Roundabout by the Bus Station, Cavan
Joey Burns

STEEL WAVES
Johnston Central Library, Farnham Street, Cavan
Edwin Lynch

THE COOTEHILL HARVESTER

Halton's Park, Cootehill

Bronze piece representing a flax-harvester. Partnership between Cootehill Building Peace Through the Arts, Cavan County Council and the Arts Council of Northern Ireland.

Tony Stallard

THE VILLAGE GREEN

Redhills

A bronze representation of a girl playing with bunting at the annual carnival. A cheerful image representing hope for a bright future for the whole community, crossing all barriers of age, diversity and religion.

Joanne Behan

Derry

THE TURFMAN
Bellaghy
Inspired by a Seamus Heaney poem: a figure fabricated in turf and then cast in bronze, celebrating Heaney's 70th birthday and his poem 'Digging'.
David Annand

BERTIE PEACOCK
The Diamond, Coleraine
Bronze statue depicting the football star who died in 2004 at the age of 75.
Ross Wilson

WAVE
St Columb's College, Buncrana Road, Derry
Maurice Harron

COLMCILLE THE SCRIBE

St Columb's College, Buncrana Road, Derry

Bronze piece dedicated to past and present pupils of the college. 'Colmcille the scribe' is a translation by former pupil Seamus Heaney of an early Irish poem, 'Sgith Mo Crob on Scribinn'. The poet did the translation to celebrate his enrolment as a member of the Royal Irish Academy in the Guildhall on 9 June 1997, the 1,400th anniversary of Colmcille's death.

Maurice Harron

JOSEF LOCKE

Queen's Quay, Derry

A bronze spiralling musical scroll with images from the life of the iconic singer, who came from the Bogside.

Maurice Harron

STEPPING OUT

Thornhill College, Culmore Road, Derry

Three abstract figures of pupils celebrating their final day at the college.

Eamon McAteer

BRONZE TILES
Rossville Street, Derry
Designed by children from Longtower Primary School facilitated by the artist, as part of the Rossville Street Environmental Improvement Scheme.
Locky Morris

THE THROW
Foyle Arena, St Columb's Park, Derry
F.E. McWilliam

THE INTERNATIONAL SAILOR
Ebrington Square, Derry
Bronze on a granite base, this is a replica of the Mariner statue in Halifax, Nova Scotia, and pays tribute to the seamen of the Allied countries who protected shipping convoys in World War II. Two Allied naval bases were built by the Americans in Derry in 1941. The barracks at Ebrington Square was handed over to the Royal Navy in the latter part of the war and was known as HMS Ferret. The sailor is carrying his hammock on his right shoulder and his kit bag in his left hand.
Peter Bustin

WINGED HORSES
Muff Road Roundabout, Derry
Artist's name unknown to the author

THE TASK—UNITY
Roundabout at St Joseph's Church, Galliagh, Derry
Stainless steel installation of four children holding aloft a diamond shape engraved with hundreds of messages from local adults and children.
Maurice Harron

CELEBRATE
Roundabout, Rath Mór shopping centre, Creggan, Derry
Five stainless steel figures of teenagers commemorating Derry City of Culture 2013.
Maurice Harron

BIRDS IN FLIGHT—SHEARWATER WAY

Brigade Road, Clooney Estate, Derry

Designed in consultation with the estate's residents, promoting the heritage of local street names.

Susan F. Hunter

1916 COMMEMORATIVE SLAB

Baile na Croise/Draperstown

Limestone piece with small Celtic knotwork, an Easter lily, an Irish poem by local poet Nóra Ní Chathain and a dedication to all who lost their lives in the 1916 Easter Rising.

Séighean Ó Draoi

FINVOLA, GEM OF THE ROE

Main Street, Dungiven

Local legend mourns the seventeenth-century Finvola, daughter of the chieftain of the O'Cahans, who married Angus McDonnell and went to live on the Isle of Islay. She died soon afterwards and her brothers sailed to Islay to bring her body home to Dungiven.

Maurice Harron

RORY DALL O'CAHAN AND THE LAMENT OF THE O'CAHAN HARP

Bleach Green entrance, Castle Park, Dungiven

Local tradition says that the original tune to *Danny Boy* came from a fairy tune heard by Rory Dall O'Cahan, a celebrated musician and O'Cahan leader in the seventeenth century.

Eleanor Wheeler and Alan Cargo

LIG-NA-PAISTE, THE LAST SERPENT IN IRELAND

Picnic Site, Feeny

Stainless steel piece on the legend that when St Patrick was driving the snakes out of Ireland one local serpent, named Lig-na-Paiste, was overlooked.

Maurice Harron

WILLIAM FERGUSON MASSEY
Council Offices, O'Connell Street, Limavady
Massey was born in Limavady in 1856, emigrated to New Zealand in 1870 and became the nineteenth prime minister of that country (1912–25).
Philip Flanagan

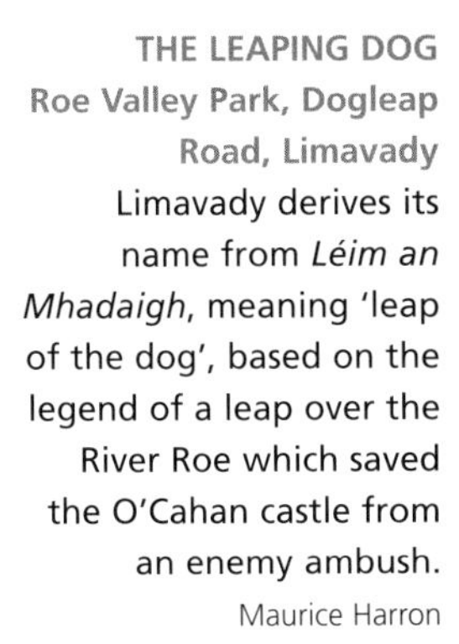

THE LEAPING DOG
Roe Valley Park, Dogleap Road, Limavady
Limavady derives its name from *Léim an Mhadaigh*, meaning 'leap of the dog', based on the legend of a leap over the River Roe which saved the O'Cahan castle from an enemy ambush.
Maurice Harron

CUSHY GLEN THE HIGHWAYMAN
Largantea Picnic Site, Windyhill Road, Limavady
Commemorates a notorious eighteenth-century highwayman who operated on this road, formerly known as Murderhole Road owing to the gruesome sights it witnessed when he preyed on his victims.
Maurice Harron

MANANNÁN MAC LIR

Gortmore Viewing Point, Binevenagh Mountain, Limavady

Local tradition tells of the presence of the Celtic sea-god Manannán in Lough Foyle: his spirit is released during fierce storms, and the waves are referred to as Manannán's sea horses.

Darren Sutton

TREES OF KILLITRA

The Loup

Five stainless steel trees, and four stone walls.

Maurice Harron

1916 PILLAR
Tirkane, Maghera
Part of a project commemorating 1916 all over Ireland by Oireachtas na Gaeilge and the Community Foundation for Ireland. They wanted to include two projects in the North, the other being in Draperstown.
Séighean Ó Draoi

OUR STORY
Market Square, Magherafelt
Globe featuring panels depicting aspects of life in the community: family, children, work, history, music and dance.
Maurice Harron

Donegal

THE THREE FATES
Herron's Field, Ardara
Three welded bronze rods, addressing the weaving heritage of the town—the bronze rod is evocative of the weaver's thread. The Three Fates are Clotho the spinner, Lachesis, who measures the thread of life with her rod, and Atropos, the cutter of the thread.
Elizabeth Caffrey

FIDDLER ON THE ROAD
The Diamond, Ardara
The fiddler John Doherty was born in Ardara.
Redmond Herrity

NATURE SEAT
Boyagh National School, Newrow, Ballindrait
Mosaic seat in three circles.
Aileen Barr

RORY GALLAGHER
Town Centre, Ballyshannon
The world-renowned rock and blues guitarist's first home was in East Port, Ballyshannon, where he was born in 1948 at the aptly named Rock Hospital.
David Annand

LIFECYCLE OF THE SALMON
Cahir O'Doherty Road, Buncrana
Mosaic surrounding a seat formed from a tree, a project carried out in conjunction with a local employment group.
Aileen Barr

SOFA
Beside the River Erne, Belleek
The sofa represents the 'way we are' aspect of the Belleek and District Partnership's Peace II Project: the homely welcome you get when visiting or returning to the village. Limestone donated by McKeon Stone and holding two time capsules: one containing history, stories and photos, and the other the dreams and wishes of local primary schoolchildren.
Stephen Burke

SUNDIAL

Lough Swilly shore, Buncrana

Tubular stainless steel gnomon with pillar stones. Delineated by Piers Nicholson and Harriet James, the gnomon was fabricated by Crana Engineering, and there is an information plaque nearby. In the background is a bust by Maurice Harron of Tip O'Neill, US Democratic politician and 47th Speaker of the House of Representatives.

JOHN NEWTON

Amazing Grace Park, Railway Road, Buncrana

Bronze of the Anglican clergyman who in his early life had worked on slave ships. After his conversion he became a prominent supporter of abolitionism and lived to see Britain's abolition of the African slave trade in 1807. He also wrote *Amazing Grace*, probably the world's most famous hymn.

Willie Malone

SALMON LEAP

Railway Road, Buncrana

Stainless steel.

Maurice Harron

THE PROMISE
An Grianán Hotel, Burt
Bronze piece depicting a Gaelic couple on their wedding day over 400 years ago, inspired by written descriptions of sixteenth-century Gaelic men and women. Travel writer Fynes Moryson wrote that the women rode side-saddle facing to the right, the opposite of the practice in England.
Maurice Harron

WARRIOR
An Grianán Hotel, Burt
Maurice Harron

CHILDREN
St Francis National School, Clonmany
Coloured steel girl and boy.
Maurice Harron

HERON
Ionad Lae, Gweedore Day Care Centre, Derrybeg
Donated by Michael Diver and his apprentices.
Gweedore FÁS Apprentices

RED HUGH O'DONNELL
Pier Area, Donegal town
Bronze piece celebrating the life and legacy of Red Hugh O'Donnell.
Maurice Harron

LUGH LÁMH FHADA
Beside Ionad Cois Locha Visitor Centre, Dunlewy
Pitch-pine totem-pole of the mythological character Lugh the sun-god, the king of the Tuatha de Danann, who led them into battle against the Fomorians. He killed his uncle, Balor of the Evil Eye, the god of darkness, in the Poison Glen. The poison from the eye gave the glen its name, according to one story. Lugh's feast, Lughnasadh, a harvest festival, was celebrated on 1 August.
Séighean Ó Draoi

	County	Carver	Stone	Motif
1.	Antrim	Fergal Donnelly	Giant's Causeway basalt	County Crest
2.	Armagh	Brian Kerrigan	Red marble	The Orchard County
3.	Carlow	Declan Nolan	Granite	The Brownshill Dolmen
4.	Cavan	Adrian Smith	Limestone	Spiral from the Killycluggin Stone
5.	Clare	Eoin Madigan	Limestone	The Poulnabrone Dolmen, music and
6.	Cork	Victor Daly	White limestone	Lettering
7.	Derry	Caite Fealty	Sandstone	The Oak Tree
8.	Donegal	Paul Phaid Cunningham	Drimkeelan sandstone	The O'Donnell Family Crest
9.	Down	Declan Grant	Mourne granite	The Ship from the County Crest
10.	Dublin	Karl Kennedy	Granite	The GPO
11.	Fermanagh	Michael Hoy	Sandstone	A trout & rabbit
12.	Galway	Christian Helling	Granite	The Claddagh
13.	Kerry	Ruairi Dennison	Kerry red marble	The Kingdom
14.	Kildare	Mickey Doherty	Limestone	The St Bridget's Cross
15.	Kilkenny	Eddie Murphy	Kilkenny black marble	Kenny's Well
16.	Laois	J. Haydon & G. Mulhall	Limestone	Lettering
17.	Leitrim	Rónán Crehan	Sandstone	Lough Allen
18.	Limerick	Colm O Brien	Blue limestone	The Galtee Mountains & castles
19.	Longford	S. May & A. Claffey	Slate	Lovers Midhir & Etain
20.	Louth	Patrick Mc Quillan	Limestone	Muiredach's High Cross
21.	Mayo	Dom Keogh	Sandstone	The Children of Lir
22.	Meath	A. Gogarty	Limestone	The Salmon of Knowledge
23.	Monaghan	Marc Kelly	White sandstone	The Tydavnet sun disc pattern
24.	Offaly	Martin Boyle	Limestone	The Easter Lily
25.	Roscommon	Michael Shanahan	Limestone	Lettering
26.	Sligo	Jamie Mc Nern	Limestone	Yeats: quill & ink
27.	Tipperary	Kenneth Curran	Sandstone	An Goban Saór by Bob Ó Cathail
28.	Tyrone	Lorcan Dunne	Sandstone	The White Hare of Creggan
29.	Waterford	Alex Panteleyenko	Sandstone	A Viking ship
30.	Westmeath	Kieran Keeney	Limestone	The Goddess Éiru
31.	Wexford	Padraig Mc Goran	Granite	A Bronze age burial urn
32.	Wicklow	Seighean Ó Draoi	Glenmalure slate	A ceathrán: an ancient sun symbol
33.	Lough Neagh	Jonathan Ball	Hand crafted glass	Waves
34.	Name plate	Michael Mc Groarty	Valentia slate	Lettering

CLOCHA NA hÉIREANN, STONES OF IRELAND
Folk Village, Glencolmcille
This collaborative piece was crafted in Irish stone to commemorate the centenary of the 1916 Rising, as part of the Tír Chonaill Stone Festival. Each county is represented by a stone carved by a native of that county.

THE RESTING SCYTHE MAN
Main Street, Gortahorc
The scythe, a farm implement used in the past for cutting hay or grass, has a long handle with a curved blade that moves parallel to the ground.
John Coll

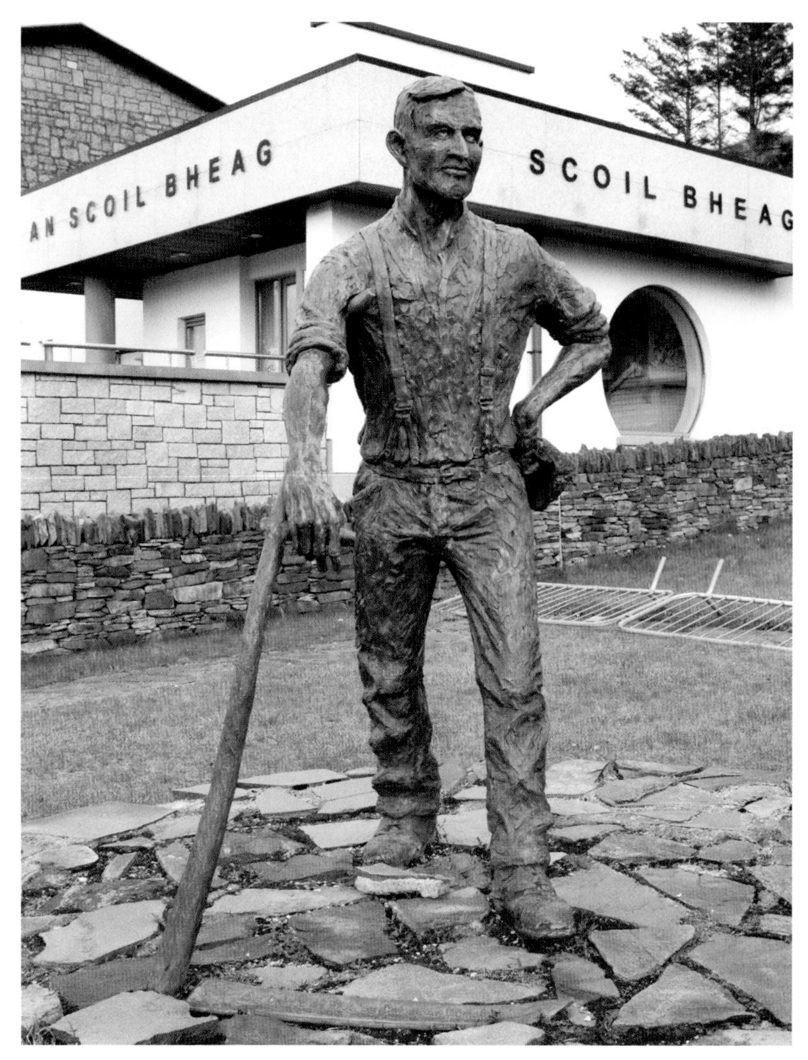

SAOIRSE CAINTE / FREEDOM OF SPEECH
Coláiste Ailigh, Cnoc na Móna, Letterkenny
With poetry by Proinsias Mac A'Bhaird, the stainless steel piece reflects the modern architecture of the building.
Fiona Mulholland

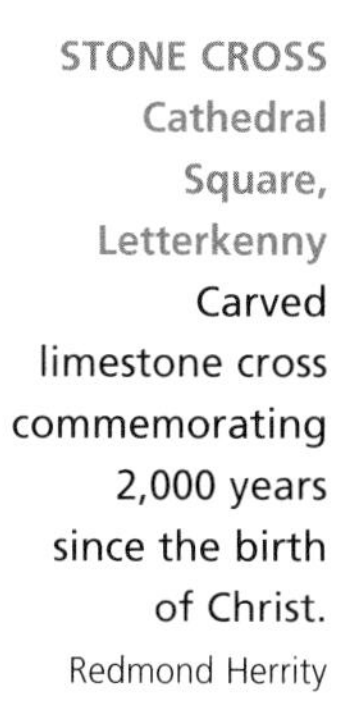

STONE CROSS
Cathedral Square, Letterkenny
Carved limestone cross commemorating 2,000 years since the birth of Christ.
Redmond Herrity

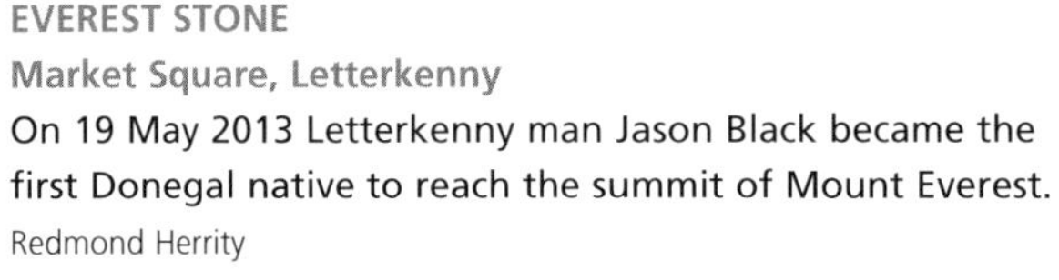

EVEREST STONE

Market Square, Letterkenny

On 19 May 2013 Letterkenny man Jason Black became the first Donegal native to reach the summit of Mount Everest.

Redmond Herrity

STANDING STONES

Mountcharles Bypass

Seven Mountcharles sandstone standing stones, uplit at night. Reinterpretation of the idea of enclosures of stones in stone circles or forts.

Gerard Harvey and Michael McGroarty

MOVILLE BENCHES
Seafront, Moville Green
Two of fifteen stone benches with carvings inspired by the local flora and fauna and the history and culture of the town.
Michael Disley

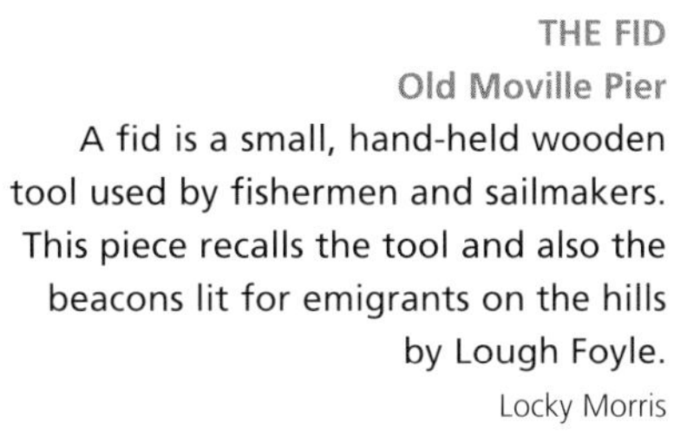

THE FID
Old Moville Pier
A fid is a small, hand-held wooden tool used by fishermen and sailmakers. This piece recalls the tool and also the beacons lit for emigrants on the hills by Lough Foyle.
Locky Morris

SHEPHERD'S CROOK
Trinity Court Day Centre, Newtowncunningham
Bronze staff symbolising the cross-community involvement in the project: the Church of Ireland, the Presbyterian Church and the Catholic Church.
Maurice Harron

ART BENCHES
Dave Gallagher Park, Ramelton
Six limestone slabs forming a series of benches, with imagery and text from the town's local history shot-blasted into the stones. The New Zealand fern symbol commemorates Dave Gallagher, who was born in Ramelton in 1873 and became the first All Blacks rugby captain, playing 36 times for New Zealand. A Boer War veteran, he was killed in action in Belgium in World War I.
Brian Connolly

THE GRAND OLD MAN OF GOLF

Rosapenna Golf Club

'Old Tom Morris', the great St Andrews golfer of the 1800s, is depicted looking out towards Sheephaven Bay. Open champion in 1861, '62, '64 and '67, he designed Rosapenna golf links in 1891.

Paul Ferriter

CELTIC CROSS SEA MEMORIAL

Seafront, Rosguil

Linda Morrison

Down

OCEAN'S EDGE
The Harbour, Ardglass
Bronze piece designed to reflect the endurance of the fishing industry in the area.
Chris Wilson

VESSEL
Phennicks Cove, Ardglass
Bronze prow of a vessel.
Alan Burke

BURR POINT
Sandylands, Ballyhalbert
Steel and bronze piece indicating the most easterly point in Ireland.
Ned Jackson Smyth

BALLYNAHINCH BELLS
Market Square, Ballynahinch
Inspired by the town's bells—within each bell are symbols of the town's story, from its early days as a crossroads to the hunt balls of Montalto House.
Paul Hogarth Company

ROMULUS AND SEAMUS
F.E. McWilliam Centre, Banbridge
The old Roman myth of Romulus and Remus being saved by a wolf is given an Irish twist.
John Kindness

CRANE
F.E. McWilliam Centre, Banbridge
Jason Ellis

FROM THE BRIDGE TO THE HILLS
Kenlis Street, Banbridge
Satin-finished stainless steel, with the cut-through pattern representing the River Bann and the outlines at the top representing the Mourne Mountains as seen from Banbridge. The artist worked with local schoolchildren to make a cast-bronze band of small tiles with patterns from the local linen industry.
Eleanor Wheeler

FLAX FLOWERS
Solitude Park, Banbridge
Reflecting the history of the linen industry in the area.
Darren Sutton

FLUCTUS ANGELORUM
Abbey Road, Bangor
Bronze bell outside the abbey church; its shape is based on the ninth-century Bangor Bell found on the site of the abbey in 1780.
Holger Lonze

SQUARE DAYS AND FAIR DAYS
Upper Square, Castlewellan
Celebrates the history of the town as a centre for markets and hiring fairs.
Alan Cargo and Eleanor Wheeler

ON THE WAY TO THE FAIR
Downpatrick Road roundabout, Clough
Stainless steel piece of a farmer bringing a cow to the fair, a common sight in this area in the past.
Darren Sutton

SPINS THE REEL, SPINS THE WHEEL
Castlewellan Road, The Lough, Corbet
This piece focuses on the industrial and cultural heritage of the linen industry. Corbet Lough was created in 1836 by the Bann Reservoir Company to aid the process of linen production.
Jason Mulligan

ST PATRICK
Belfast Road, Downpatrick
Stainless steel abstract of the saint, with the town's name included.
Melanie Jackson

DOWNPATRICK HIGH CROSS
Roughal Park, Downpatrick
Multifaceted cast-aluminium interpretation of the Celtic high cross.
Bob Sloan

THE SILENT DOG
Scotch Street, Downpatrick
Commemorating the work of author Lynn C. Doyle, who was born in the town. The figures of Mr Harrington, Mr Anthony, Pat and the 'silent' dog feature in one of his short stories.
David Annand

THE PENANNULAR BROOCH
St Patrick's Centre, Downpatrick
Large bronze representation of the brooches used to fasten cloaks in the Early Christian period.
Alan Burke

STRUELL WELLS SPRING STONE
Downe Hospital, Struell Wells Road, Downpatrick
Marie Brett

HARRY FERGUSON
Dromore
Ferguson leaning on a gate beside the old family home. He was the inventor of the modern tractor and the integrated plough-hitch attachment. He also invented the four-wheel drive system used in Formula One cars and landrovers, and in 1909 he designed, built and flew the first monoplane.
John Sherlock

TONN RURAY SCULPTURE HORN
Dundrum
The 'tonn ruray' is the mythical wave associated with Dundrum. The piece is covered with historical texts and images relating to the village.
Killen and McKenna

BLAEBERRY SUNDAY
Peter Morgan's Cottage, Finnis
Marking the annual 'Blaeberry Sunday' walk to the summit of Slieve Croob.
Jason Mulligan

HARRY FERGUSON'S MONOPLANE
M1 at Ballygowan Road
Stainless steel image of the inventor—whose first flight took place near Hillsborough—about to land the monoplane that he designed, built and flew in 1909.
John Sherlock

JOHNNY THE JIG

High Street, Holywood

Bronze figure of a boy playing the accordion, commemorating the death in 1952 of local boy scout Fergus Morton, who was killed in a road accident while out on bob-a-job fund-raising.

Sophia Rosamund Praeger

A PONY, A PUMP, AND TWO GENTLEMEN WHO NEVER MET

The Square, Hilltown

This spot was once the site of a pump where the locals gathered to chat.

Ralf Sander

THE MOURNE HAND
Silent Valley Mountain Park, Head Road, Kilkeel
The inspiration for this piece came from sources in the area—the Silent Valley reservoir and dam, and the Binnian Tunnel—and the hand at the base represents the Mourne men who built them.
Richard Janes

COMMON GROUND
Derriaghy Village Community Association, Lisburn
Cast bronze; a Building Peace Through the Arts public art commission.
Mark Ryan and Maree Hensey

LANDMARKS
Tollymore National Outdoor Centre, Bryansford, Newcastle
Consists of displaced sections suggesting stone slabs, with contour map details of mountains, rivers, pathways and text. It includes miniature climbing figures to highlight the huge scale of the mountains.
Chris Wilson

WIND AND SEA
Slieve Donard, Downs Road, Newcastle
Bronze piece featuring two back-to-back dancing figures, sculpted in Florence and representing the harmony between wind and sea.
Patrick Campbell

LIBERTE
Slieve Donard, Newcastle
Liberte means 'freedom' in Italian—freedom to celebrate life, as expressed in the joyful figure of this young woman.
Patrick Campbell

THE SMUGGLER'S HEAD
Bloody Bridge, Ballagh Road, Newcastle
Refers to the age-old custom of smuggling. At the correct angle, the outline of the smuggler's head becomes visible between the two columns.
Ralf Sander

LISTENER OF THE SEA
Newcastle seafront
One of a series of sculptures depicting a seaside theme and named by local schoolchildren.
Alan Burke

TAILS OF FLIGHT
Newcastle promenade

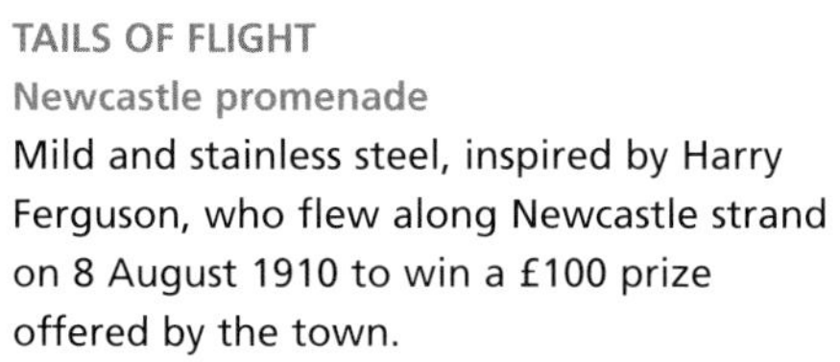

Mild and stainless steel, inspired by Harry Ferguson, who flew along Newcastle strand on 8 August 1910 to win a £100 prize offered by the town.

Charles Normandale

STARFISH
Newcastle seafront
Alan Burke

TRADING PLACE
Buttercrane Quay, Bridge Street junction, Newry
Bronze piece whose front suggests the prow of a boat or barge, referencing the histories of transport and trade that contributed to the city's development. The front shows various goods traded in Newry, the middle indicates the canal, and the highest section reflects the buildings and warehouses resulting from Newry's trading success.
Chris Wilson

THE PROUD PEOPLE
Marcus Square, Newry
Installed in 1994 to commemorate 850 years of Newry history. The title comes from a description of the town by Jonathan Swift: 'high church, low steeple, dirty streets, proud people'.
Patrick McElroy

THE NEWRY DOCKER
Albert Basin, Newry
Bronze piece of a working docker in this area. The Newry docks closed in 1976.
Tony Stallard

HATS FOR HEROES
Marcus Square, Newry
Mark Ryan and Maree Hensey

THE NEWRY NAVVY
Sugar Island Bridge, Newry
Bronze piece celebrating the men who built the Newry Canal which was completed in 1742. The original canal labourers were called navigators, later shortened to 'navvy', a term associated worldwide with Irish labourers.
Barry Linnane

PATRICK RANKIN
Dublin Bridge, Newry
The Newry man cycled 70 miles from Down to Dublin to take part in the 1916 Easter Rising and was based in the GPO during the battle.
Barry Linnane

THE TOWER OF IMAGINATION

A1 Dublin/Belfast, Newry

Stainless steel structure with a series of images and themes of children, houses and castles—with animals and friendly monsters peering out of the windows.

Maurice Harron

JOHN MITCHEL

St Colman's Park, Hill Street, Newry

The patriot and founder of the publication *The United Irishman* was born in 1815 and grew up in Newry. Sentenced to fourteen years for treason, he escaped to the United States, where he published his famous prison memoir, *Jail Journal*.

Domhnall Ó Murchadha

LUCK PENNY

Market Square, Rathfriland

Relates to the town's connection with markets and in particular to the practice of giving back a penny for luck when a deal was sealed. Images of the products sold at the markets are shown on the surface, with a large bronze 'luck penny' as the centre-piece.

Eleanor Wheeler

SUSTRANS
Scarva
Bronze and stone, one of a series of installations on the Portadown/Newry Canal for the Sustrans Cycle Network.
Niall Walsh

THE IRISH ELK
Narrow Water roundabout, Warrenpoint
Life-size stainless steel figure of an Irish elk, which had the largest antlers of any member of the deer family.
Clare Bigger and Paul Regan

Fermanagh

WAITING
Railway Station, Brookeborough
Railway sleepers carved to resemble waiting figures, with small bronzes attached. Some of these bronzes have regrettably left home!
Amanda Montgomery

GROWING TOGETHER
Larganess Centre, Florencecourt, Enniskillen
The inspiration for this piece came from the famous Florencecourt yew tree, planted nearby in the 1700s from a sapling found on the Cuilcagh Mountain. It is still growing today and is referred to as the Mother Tree. It is believed that most of the Irish yew trees grown in churchyards all over the world came from this one tree. The project was supported by the Building Peace Through the Arts programme.
Kevin Killen

CARROSYL FOR PEACE

Carrowshee Park, Lisnaskea

The piece is a symbol of inclusion, representing those in all the estates that make up the area, and relates to the connections between the people, the heritage and the diversity of Carrosyl. The project was supported by the Building Peace Through the Arts programme.

Mark Ryan and Maree Hensey

TOPPED MOUNTAIN, ENNISKILLEN

Holger Lonze

ALL HELL BY TOPPED'S GATE

Signpost.

TOPPED MOUNTAIN, ENNISKILLEN

MINIATURE BRONZE BELLS
Coolbuck church grounds
Mini-bells made using Bronze Age outdoor casting and firing techniques.
Holger Lonze with Topped Mountain Community Association and local artists

COOLBUCK BELL
Coolbuck church
Bronze bell.

Monaghan

ST MAELDOID'S PIG
N2 Dublin/Derry at Castleblayney
In the sixth century St Maeldoid tried to build a monastery at Concra, on one side of Lough Muckno, but a black pig repeatedly took the stones to Churchill on the lake's east side. The monastery was eventually built in Churchill and the ruins still stand there.
David Annand

THE NEST
Hope Castle, Castleblayney
A symbolic piece that compares Castleblayney to a bird's nest, a home where life begins and growth is nurtured.
Compass Northglass

BIG TOM
Town centre, Castleblayney
Tom McBride was a well-known Irish country singer and guitarist, whose musical career began in the 1960s with the showband Big Tom and the Mainliners.
Mark Richards

RED RAIN
The Market House, Monaghan
In this stained-glass piece on the northern side of the building the drumlins of Monaghan blend and metamorphose from landscape to townscape.
Peadar Lamb

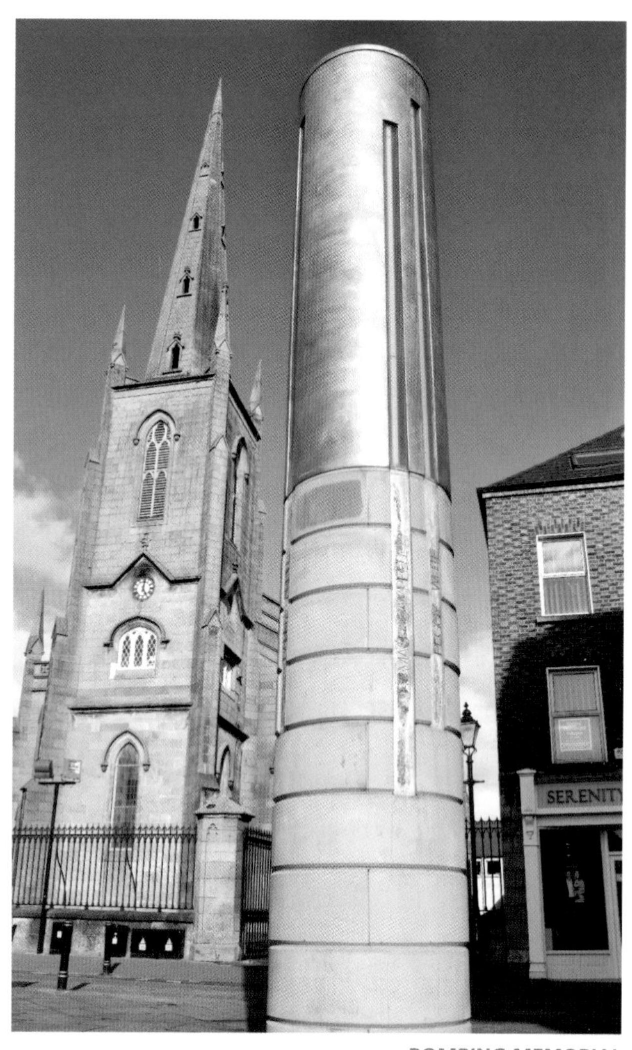

BOMBING MEMORIAL
Courthouse, Monaghan
On 17 May 1974 a series of coordinated bombings took place, three in Dublin during rush hour and one in Monaghan soon afterwards—the deadliest attacks of the entire Northern Ireland Troubles. Thirty-three people and a full-term unborn baby died, and almost 300 were injured.
Ciaran Ó Cearnaigh

MOVING ON

Ulster Canal Greenway, Coolshanagh Roundabout, Monaghan

Stainless steel and cast bronze, representing the role of the canal in the region's history. The sense of movement in the piece, owing to its curved and balanced elements, relates to the Ulster Canal once facilitating the movement of goods, animals and people in the region. A Building Peace Through the Arts public art commission.

Mark Ryan and Maree Hensey

HIVE OF KNOWLEDGE

Courthouse, Monaghan

Commissioned for the International Forge-In held here in June 2011 as part of the 'Year of Craft'. The hive was designed to hold panels crafted during the weekend by fifteen artist blacksmiths assisted by over 120 other blacksmiths from all over the world, with the largest collection of anvils ever assembled. Spending the weekend watching this extraordinary celebration of blacksmithing was an unforgettable experience.

Mark Keeling

Tyrone

MADONNA AND CHILD
Servite Priory, Benburb
Gabriel Hayes

CONVERGENCE
Benburb
Bronze sculpture inspired by the archaeology and industrial heritage of the Blackwater River, which marks the boundary between Armagh and Tyrone.
Holger Lonze

FISH MOSAIC
King George V recreational area, Campsie
Ceramic piece on a stretch of wall overlooking the Camowen River. Includes salmon, flowers and a girl on a swing, representing the river, local flora and the children's playpark.
Gerry Bradley

GATHERING POTATOES
Campsie Park
Two people, one digging and the other collecting the potatoes in a bucket.
Dara Hand

TIMELINE
Market Square, Dungannon
This bronze piece takes the viewer on a journey: it uses the form of ancient Irish gold lunulae and penannular brooches to create an arc shape linking the past and the present through ancient and modern patterns and designs.

Chris Wilson

MAKE A WISH

Community House, Drumragh Avenue, Omagh

Cast/fabricated bronze, optic fibre, LED lighting and No. 7 interior lighting elements. This piece commemorates the victims of the 1998 IRA bombing of the Community House—the building in the background. The artist chose the image of a dandelion because it encapsulates the beauty and fragility of life. The piece incorporates a series of seeds placed inside the building, which when viewed from outside appear to be floating as if they had been scattered.

Alex Pentek

OMAGH PEACE GARDEN

Drumragh Road and Market Street, Omagh

The large mirrors at the memorial garden track the sun by computer and direct the sunlight via the 31 smaller mirrors, representing the lives lost in the explosion, down the street, where another group of mirrors bend the light around the corner and finally, via one small mirror, onto the heart of the six-ton glass pillar.

Seán Hillen and Desmond Fitzgerald

WAR MEMORIAL
Town centre, Castlederg
Commemorating those who died in both World Wars.
Philip Flanagan

MYLES AFTER MYLES
The Library and Arts Centre, Railway Street, Strabane
Sculpture commemorating the novelist, playwright and satirist Brian O'Nolan, a major figure in twentieth-century Irish literature, who was born in Strabane in 1911. He wrote under the pen-names of Myles na gCopaleen and Flann O'Brien.
Holger Lonze

EMIGRANTS' WALL
Bowling Green, Strabane
Cast-bronze and carved sandstone wall containing the names of famous Strabane emigrants.
Bob Sloan

Iconic images

ICONIC IMAGES

I decided to close my collection of sculptures with two images that were temporarily located in Dublin in November 2018, shortly before I completed my work on the book. Because many people would not be in a position to see these two iconic installations, I thought it would be nice to share them.

THE FEARLESS GIRL

The statue with the motto 'Know the power of women in leadership' symbolises female leadership and workplace gender diversity. For International Women's Day 2017 the feisty 1.4m girl was controversially placed defiantly facing Arturo Di Modica's colossal Charging Bull of Wall Street. The statue was brought to Dublin in support of the country's first Climate Week in November 2018.

Kristen Visbal

THE HAUNTING SOLDIER

This image is included to commemorate the centenary of the end of World War I. The 6m-high installation—created from scrap metal pieces, including car jacks, spanners, horseshoes, brake discs and bicycle parts—was on display in Dublin's St Stephen's Green during November 2018. The Armistice was signed at 11.00am on the eleventh day of the eleventh month in 1918.

Dublin-based solicitor Sabina Purcell came across photos of the sculpture, and when she discovered that she has a family connection with WWI she decided to arrange the temporary move to Ireland.

Artist blacksmith Martin Galbavy and Chris Hannam of Dorset Forge and Fabrication

INDEX OF SCULPTORS

Mick Clifford,

Fiona Coffey,

John Coll,

Jim Collins,

Brendan Collum,

Compass Northglass,

Fred Conlon,

Nigel Connell Bass,

Angela Conner,

Brian Connolly,

Jim Connolly,

Robert Connolly,

Seamus Connolly,

Jerome Connor,

Agnes Conway,

Kris Copeland,

Alan Counihan,

Martina Coyle,

Tommy Craggs,

Don Cronin,

Crowley Brothers,

Philip Cullen,

Marjorie Cunningham,

Pat Cunningham,

Cliodna Cussen,

D

Jarlath Daly,

Paul D'Arcy,

Orla de Brí,

Róisín de Buitléar,

Remco de Fouw,

Deiseal (Antony Lyons, Niall O'Neill and Holger Lonze),

Edward Delaney,

R. Dennison,

Paul Devlin,

Marc Didou,

Michael Disley,

Michael Diver and FÁS apprentices,

Laury Dizengremel,

Carmel Doherty,

Ken Drew,

Peadar Drinan,

Gary Duffy,

Ana Duncan,

Michael Duhan,

Seamus Dunbar,

E

James Earley,

Dan Edwards,

Jason Ellis,

Clodagh Emoe,

Eoin (Art by Eoin),

F

Orlagh Fahy,

Conor Fallon,

Catherine Fanning,

Steve Feeny,

Kevin Fennelly,

Marisa Ferreira,

Paul Ferriter,

Paul Finch,

Barry Finnegan,

Desmond Fitzgerald,

Philip Flanagan,

Jim Flavin,

Paul Flynn,

Will Fogarty,

Michael Foley,

Mel French,

G

Martin Galbavy,

Alva Gallagher,

James Gannon,

Mark Garry,

Elaine Gavin,

Moss Gaynor, Mojo,

Conleth Gent,

Dan George,

Abdul Ghofur,

Rowan Gillespie,

Hillary Gilligan,

Mary Gilmore,

Shane Gilmore,

Thomas Glendon,

Raymond Glynn,

Yann Renard Goulet,

Peter Grant,

Catherine Greene,

Lara Greene,

Paul Gregg,

Colin Grehan,

Elaine Griffin,

H

Brian Halpin,

Ronan Halpin,

Dara Hand,

Chris Hannam,

Hugh Hanratty,

Caoilfhionn Hanton,

Alan Hall,

Maurice Harron,

Gerard Harvey,

Gabriel Hayes,

James Hayes,

John Hayes,

Richie Healy,

Maree Hensey,

Martin Heron,

Alan Beattie Herriott,

Redmond Herrity,

Adrienne Heslin,

Leo Higgins,

Seán Hillen,

Joseph Hillier,

Peter Hodnett,

John Hogan,

Paul Hogarth Company,

Kevin Holland,

Shane Holland,

Fred Hoppe,

James Horan,

Jon Barlow Hudson,

Ann Meldon Hugh,

Susan F. Hunter,

I

IABA: Irish Artist Blacksmiths Association,

J

Melanie Jackson,

Ngaire Jackson,

Harriet James,

Richard Janes,

Michael Johnson,

Colin Johnston,

Dick Joynt,

Rachel Joynt,

K

Orla Kaminska,

Mark Keeling,

Áine Kelly,

John Kelly,

Oisín Kelly,

Mike Kenny,

Pamela Keogh,

Jonathan Kerr,

Cathail Kierans,

Kevin Killen,

Michael Killen,

Killen and McKenna,

John Kindness,

Brian King,

Lynn Kirkham,

Tiiu Kirsipuu,

Vera Klute,

Pieter Koning,

Cornelia Konrads,

Henk Korthuys,

Nickhola Kyle,

L

Peadar Lamb,

Larne Skills Development,

Liam Lavery,

Clare Lawson,

Lloyd Le Blanc,

Billy Leen,

Mary Leen,

Dan Leonard,

Gerard Leslie,

Barry Linnane,

Anika Linterman,

Peter Logan,

Holger Lonze,

Éamon Looney,

Hugh Lorigan,

Patrick Loughran,

Edwin Lynch,

Antony Lyons,

Martin Lyttle,

M

Cathy MacAleavey,
Éamon McAteer,
Patrick McAuliffe,
Aoife McCarrick,
Caroline McCarthy,
Cathal McCarthy,
Dan McCarthy,
James McCarthy,
Seán McCarthy,
Billy McCaughern,
Dermot McConaghy,
Annette McCormack,
Emma McDermott,
Heather McDermott,
Eileen MacDonagh,
Maurice McDonagh,
Patrick McElroy,
Brendan McGloinn,
Michael McGroarty,
Christine Mackay,
Jackie McKenna,
James McKenna,
Jerry McKenna,
Sally McKenna,
Micheál McKeown,
Jimmy Joe McKiernan,
Elizabeth McLaughlin,
James McLoughlin,
Kevin McMahon,
Dony MacManus,
Joseph McNally,
Eleonora McNamara,
Joe McNamara,
Austin McQuinn,
Michael McTigue,
F.E. McWilliam,
Betty Newman Maguire,
Willie Malone,
Mantra,
Shiro Masuyama,
Laurent Mellet,
Kieran Melody,
Walter Michael,
Mick Minogue,
Barry Moloney,
John Monaghan,
Micky Monaghan,
Amanda Montgomery,
Locky Morris,
Patrick Morris,
Linda Morrison,
Jane Mortimer,
Gordon Muir,
Gerard Mulhall,
Fiona Mulholland,
Nigel Mullan,
Jason Mulligan,
Thomas Mulloy,
Ann Mulrooney,
D.V. Murngan,

Anne Murphy,

Fiona Murphy,

Seamus Murphy,

Conor Murray,

Paddy Murray,

Jane Murtagh,

N

Joe Neeson,

Piers Nicholson,

Edain Ní Dhómhnaill,

Bríd Ní Rínn,

Charles Normandale,

Tanya Nyegaard,

O

Don O'Boyle,

Ciaran O'Brien,

Colette O'Brien,

Ray O'Callaghan,

Ciaran Ó Cearnaigh,

Eilis O'Connell,

Pauline O'Connell,

Andrew O'Connor,

Denis O'Connor,

John O'Connor,

Éamonn O'Doherty,

Marion O'Donnell,

Tighe O'Donoghue Ross,

Séighean Ó Draoi,

Paul O'Driscoll,

Fiona O'Dwyer,

Kevin O'Dwyer,

Neil O'Dwyer,

Elizabeth O'Kane,

Martin O'Keefe,

Niall O'Lochlainn,

Patrick O'Loughlin,

John O'Mahony,

John O'Malley,

Tony O'Malley,

Dómhnall Ó Murchadha,

Eric O'Neill,

Farhad Nargol O'Neill,

Liam O'Neill,

Niall O'Neill,

Cormac O'Reilly,

Patrick O'Reilly,

Danny Osborne,

Paula O'Sullivan,

Susan O'Toole,

P

Paul Page,

Alejandro Pakarati,

Carl Payne,

Alex Pentek,

Richard Perry,

Sophia Rosamund Praeger,

Des Prendergast,

Patsy Preston,

Travis Price,

Q

Michael Quane,

Mark Quilligan,

Bob Quinn,

Martha Quinn,

Tina Quinn,

R

Skelton Rainey,

Patrick Randall,

Pádraic Reaney,

Paul Regan,

Mark Richards,

Fritze Rind,

Eithne Ring,

Malcolm Robertson,

Mark Rode,

Cillian Rogers,

Peter Rooney,

John Rowlands,

Christopher Ryan,

Mark Ryan,

Jeanne Rynhart,

S

Ralf Sander,

William Sandham,

James Scanlan,

Valli Schafer,

Timothy Schmalz,

Anthony Scott,

Noel Scullion,

Sebastian,

A.J. Victor Segoffin,

Bettina Seitz,

Jethro Sheen,

John Sherlock,

Bob Sloan,

Fifi Smith,

Mike Smith,

Paki Smith,

Ned Jackson Smyth,

Alexander Sokolov,

Sonny,

Tony Stallard,

Ian Stuart,

Imogen Stuart,

Darren Sutton,

Brian Swan,

Catherine Synnott,

T

Pat Taaffe,

Therese and Debbie Tierney,

Ken Thompson,

Emer Toomey

Gary Trimble,

Jim Turner,

V

Ron van der Noll,

Brigitta Varadi,

Kristen Visbal,

W

Joe and Pat Walker,

Joseph Walsh,

Killian Walsh,

Niall Walsh,

Brendan Walshe,

Tim Ward,

Michael Warren,

Alexandra Wejchert,

Pamela Wells,

Elke Westen,

Eleanor Wheeler,

Michael Whelan,

Julian Wild,

Wild Metal,

Mick Wilkins,

Gwen Wilkinson,

Chris Wilson,

Ross Wilson,

Barry Wrafter,

Daphne Wright,

X

Shen Xiaonan,

Y

Zhang Yaxi,

Z

ZAP Architecture,

Giorgio Zennaro,